Fiddler on the Move

AMERICAN MUSICSPHERES

Series Editor
Mark Slobin

The Lord's Song in a Strange Land
Music and Identity in Contemporary Jewish Worship
Jeffrey A. Summit

Fiddler on the Move
Exploring the Klezmer World
Mark Slobin

FIDDLER ON THE MOVE

Exploring the Klezmer World

Mark Slobin

UNIVERSITY PRESS

2000

OXFORD
UNIVERSITY PRESS
Oxford   New York
Athens   Auckland   Bangkok   Bogotá   Buenos Aires   Calcutta
Cape Town   Channai   Dar es Salaam   Delhi   Florence   Hong Kong   Istanbul
Karachi   Kuala Lumpur   Madrid   Melbourne   Mexico City   Mumbai
Nairobi   Paris   São Paulo   Shanghai   Singapore   Taipei   Tokyo   Toronto   Warsaw

and associated companies in
Berlin   Ibadan

Copyright © 2000 by Oxford University Press, Inc.

Published by Oxford University Press
198 Madison Avenue, New York, New York 10016

Oxford is a registered trademark of Oxford University Press.

Library of Congress Cataloging-in-Publication Data
Slobin, Mark
Fiddler on the move : exploring the klezmer world / Mark Slobin.
p. cm.—(American musicspheres)
Includes bibliographical references and index.
ISBN 0-19-513124-X
1. Klezmer music—History and criticism.
2. Jews—Music—History and criticism.
I. Title. II. Series
ML3528.8 .S58 2000
781.62'924—dc21   99-048683
Cover photograph: posters on a wall in Budapest, 1999.
Used by permission of Ruth Gruber.

1 3 5 7 9 8 6 4 2
Printed in the United States of America
on acid-free paper

For
my favorite
Keshenever shtikele
_____

Foreword

Spheres within spheres—this is what American music looks like in the early twenty-first century. Overlapping, intersecting, sharp at the core and fuzzy at the edges: large and small music systems surround Americans and project the region's sound to the world. This is a multidimensional, surprising set of worlds in collision. The machinery of marketing and media struggle to straighten out the shapes, styles, and meanings. Tinges of domination, accommodation, and reciprocity color the picture.

"America" here means the several cultural spaces that center on the United States, both magnet and generator of musical energy. This nation-state once understood its musical map as an overlay of "white" on "black," with "color" added by continuous overlays of absorbed populations, some brought in by aggressive territorial expansion, others by the pull of immigration or the push of disaster. It took the whole twentieth century to shift to a more nuanced sense of internal cultural ferment. Now we can see any musician or audience as an influencer or receptor. Groups actively seek to control their own definition, often consciously crossing cultural and national borders. The media both empower and disempower musical taste and direction through target marketing.

This series will present concise, focused accounts of a sampling of spheres. Some studies will describe a localized group, but show how a micromusic is implicated in broad trends and constantly changing ways of thinking about musical choices. Some books survey "networks," circuits of sensibility that bind people regionally or nationally. Others will introduce an individual as a prism that refracts and breaks down the harsh beam of American life into an intensely hued pattern of musical light. Yet others might seize on a musical moment of particular intensity.

The overall aim: to avoid defining musical "villages," to move away from neat periodization, and to give terms like "folk," "traditional," "ethnic," and "popular" a well-deserved rest. American music studies needs new perspectives; this series hopes to suggest some.

MARK SLOBIN
Series Editor
American Musicspheres

Acknowledgments

I would like to acknowledge the generosity of many klezmer colleagues over the years, who have freely shared their insights and their brilliant, moving musicianship. In the early years, Ethel Raim and Martin Koenig were kind enough to invite me on the first Dave Tarras tour. Henry Sapoznik was a distinctive early voice. Michael Alpert and Zev Feldman have been generous interlocutors. Most recently, Hankus Netsky's exceptional range of knowledge and insight and his willingness to experiment with a Wesleyan klezmer band pushed me to the work before you. Alicia Svigals and Deborah Strauss have taught me a great deal about current klezmer, and Kurg Bjorling's reissue of old materials and Martin Schwartz's work have put us all in their debt. From the time in 1973 when she enlisted me into Yiddish culture studies, Barbara Kirshenblatt-Gimblett has been a steady partner in a long-running dialogue. Chana Mlotek and the staff of the YIVO Institute for Jewish Research have always been a source of inspiration and moral support. Greta's spontaneous enthusiasm for the music has made this a joint voyage of discovery, deepening the experience immeasurably.

I am grateful to Wesleyan University for the sabbatical year 1997–98, funding for the Wesleyan Klezmer Research Conference of 1996, and frequent sabbaticals and unpaid leaves over the nearly thirty years of my tenure there. This is also the right moment to thank the thinkers of the University of California at Santa Cruz, where I spent a good portion of my time while bicoastally commuting, and where the Center for Cultural Studies, in the heady days of James Clifford's leadership, offered terrific stimulation. I would also like to thank the Music Department of UCSC for routinely arranging a Research Associate status, which has allowed me to plug in to the local campus resources, and Fred Lieberman for sonogramic colleagueship.

Contents

Fiddler on the Move

Two major klezmer bands of the 1990s. Svigals, Strauss, Netsky, and Bressler are cited extensively in this book.

Top: The Klezmatics: *clockwise from right:* Alicia Svigals, Frank London, David Licht, Paul Morrissett, Matt Darlau, Lorin Sklamberg.

Bottom: Klezmer Conservatory Band: *top row, left to right:* Mark Hamilton, Art Bailey, Jeff Warschauer, Robin Miller. *Second row:* Jim Guttman, Deborah Strauss, Hankus Netsky, Ilene Stahl, Mark Berney. *Front row:* Judy Bressler, Grant Smith.

1

Under the Klezmer Umbrella

A Russian folktale, retold by Mirra Ginsburg as a children's book, narrates the arrival, one by one, of a series of animals looking for shelter from the rain under a mushroom. By book's end, the question is: how could so many of them fit under a mushroom? The answer, of course, is that mushrooms grow in the rain. "Klezmer" is a modern musical mushroom that seems to have magical powers which are not discussed by Ginsburg's childhood model but are well-known to hip adults. Over the last two and a half decades, many musicians have discovered this uncontrolled substance and have created an aesthetic, sometimes communal, vision hovering between a homeland to a happening for themselves and for audiences from Minsk to Melbourne.

I happened to be around when the mushroom was feeling the first raindrops that would cause its enormous expansion. In 1977, just as the first two or three "klezmer" albums were turning up in record stores, two pioneer activists, Walter Zev Feldman and Andy Statman, formed an alliance with the reluctant old master Dave Tarras, to offer what was perceived as a past music to a present audience. I was the academic "presenter" put on to legitimize their project for the granting agencies and the Balkan Arts Center, the New York sponsor. We went to Orange, New Jersey, to play for a Jewish community that was not supposed to be interested in this rerunning of old tunes, and the place was full. We visited Co-op City, refuge for a generation of Jews who had been uprooted by master planner Robert Moses's destruction of their neighborhood to build the Cross-Bronx Expressway. Some 1,500 gray-haired listeners mobbed the place, later reminding Tarras that he had played at their wedding decades before. Meanwhile, new bands were springing up in key locations in the United States. The music's stimulus seemed to find receptors in the communal nervous system of American Jewry, jumping across generational neural gaps.

Even the early phase of this refocusing on the klezmer heritage was complex, but only if you were surprised by the power of American music to recombine and redefine itself. If so, you might be amazed at the sudden appearance of the Klezmer Conservatory Band, in 1979, an experiment by Hankus Netsky, a faculty member at the staid New England Conservatory. At their concerts, Don Byron, an African American, held forth on clarinet, alternately stroking and tweaking the Jewish-American audience's nerves, and the trumpeter was a blonde, non-Jewish woman. They played curious material no one had heard before, like Lt. Joseph Frankel's 1919 "Yidishe Blues," one of the earliest jazz-influenced pieces by any recording group of that time (let alone by a Jewish lieutenant), and hardly the kind of piece you would program if you were looking for Old World nostalgia, which Netsky clearly wasn't. This was American music indeed, with all the unexpected interchanges and off-ramps on the musical highway, where the traffic followed its own individualist logic while moving ahead in packs like bands of bikers.

I was intrigued, and by 1984 I had written a couple of reviews and articles on the burgeoning klezmer movement, which even then seemed to include a really unusual range of musicians who kept crowding under the mushroom after leaving happy musical homes in other parts of the American musical forest. Some arrived from jazz, some from bluegrass and old-time styles, others from Balkan and folk backgrounds. These players became proselytizers, converting many others to a new sensibility centered on "heritage" in the wake of the great bicentennial recognition of what came to be called multiculturalism.

A high point of early activism was the foundation in 1985 of KlezKamp, then associated with the YIVO Institute for Jewish Research, a steadfast champion of the cultural heritage of the Eastern European Jews who formed 90 percent of American Jewry. In a run-down hotel in the Catskills, that legendary utopia of working-class Jewish leisure, Henry Sapoznik organized a klezmer institute at Christmastime, challenging Jews to de-camp from their assimilationist holiday making to immerse themselves in the Yiddish tradition. The small group of us that arrived to teach and learn rattled around the knotty-pine interior of the Paramount Hotel in Parksville, New York.

I moved on to several other projects and, ten years later, turned around to look at what had happened to the klezmer scene. I was amazed. There were developments that would have caused roars of incredulous laughter in the halls of the Paramount. When I returned to KlezKamp in 1996, it had expanded to 450 people of all ages and persuasions (ranging from Orthodox to members of New York's "queer" scene). Meanwhile klezmer had spread across Europe, to the avant-garde "downtown" music world of New York City, and up to the highest spheres of classical music, violin superstar Itzhak Perlman. As an ethnomusicologist, I felt challenged by this moment of surprise. It reminded me of a 1977 convention paper by Alan Merriam, a scholar and one of the modern founders of my field, ethnomusicology. Merriam had returned to Africa after many years of absence to find that "his people" had moved in unanticipated musical directions. He publicly asked his audience to help him understand what had happened. Impressed that such a formidable thinker could make such a move, I learned that surprise is part of the research process.

I began to travel the klezmer highways and byways to figure out the changes in klezmer. Things were so molten in the mid-1990s that it was hard to find my methodological footing. My work ranged from interviews to my initiation as a klezmer fiddler at the hands of Hankus Netsky, now my graduate student. It seemed that a book on this topic should bring a set of essays under a conceptual umbrella: klezmerology, or, how to study a constantly morphing and expanding musical system with no surviving homeland, as played by insiders with outsider mentalities and outsiders with uncanny intuitions about how the music works. I've chosen several angles from which to view this teeming scene of concerts and CDs rather than offering a coherent history or a comprehensive survey. Several perspectives have come to mind, and they shape the remaining chapters of this book. The sources, examples, and insights intersect, jumping the temporary fences I've put up to suggest methodological territories.

Klezmer as a heritage music: Viewed one way, klezmer has a core that is distinctive and sometimes unique, but at its edges it overlaps a large set of musical systems that have come to be called "heritage musics." So to understand how klezmer works, it seems unavoidable to do an overhead shot of these restless yet rooted music-making contexts.

Klezmer as an urge: Perhaps there are driving forces that span the extraordinary variety of transatlantic klezmer activities. What moves musicians and excites audiences to embrace klezmer?

Klezmer as community: Although the music is mobile, bands and audiences tend to be grounded in specific environments. Players and payers are united by an interest in building a common vision of what klezmer is or might be. This chapter unfolds the concept of the "klezmer community."

Klezmer style as a statement: Listening, not just looking, yields a steady stream of insights into any micromusical evolution. Leaning on the approaches of tune biography, individual legacy, and stylistic detail, this chapter suggests ways that sensibilities have shaped style over the decades, stressing selected current performers' outlooks.

The Fiddler's Farewell: closing thoughts before packing up and moving on.

Having mapped out my own, and this book's, itinerary, let me step back and explain what I mean by "klezmer." I use it as a noun to refer to a field of music-making, although the original Yiddish word covers only the person, the professional musician as a specialized member of a close-knit Ashkenazic community over the last few centuries. I also refer to musicians as "klezmer" or "klezmorim" (the Yiddish plural, though *klezmer* or *klezmers* can also be used as a plural noun). Yiddish does not offer a term such as *klezmer-muzik* for what musicians played, perhaps because they adjusted to consumer demand rather than staying within a restricted repertoire. "Klezmer music" was coined in English around 1980 in the United States to cover the preferences of an emerging group of activists who defined a new system based on a variety of resources. Klezmorim among themselves do use "klezmer" in this generalized way, so it's something of an insider's term, but it is also the way record stores classify their albums. This usage allows you to say "Where's the klezmer bin?" or "Klezmer has spread to Italy," a shorthand way to refer a social phenomenon that covers much more than music.

I will not undertake a history of klezmer here, but a telescoped summary does seem helpful.[1] As a cultural keyword, klezmer belongs to the world of the eastern Ashkenazic Jews, a branch of world Jewry that, according to the standard account, crystalized slowly, starting about a thousand years ago around the Franco-German borderlands. There, Jews from a variety of geographic and cultural backgrounds developed what came to be called "Yiddish," one of the many internal languages Jews have developed wherever they settled. In their capacity as middlemen, the Jews migrated ever farther east, infiltrating the Slavic lands over the next few hundred years. At the end of the eighteenth century the largest population of Jews in the world was absorbed into the Russian Empire as the Russian, Prussian, and Austrian Empires carved up the kingdom of Poland. The Russian approach was to draw a line around an absorbed people and tell them to stay there; the zone is called in English the Pale of Settlement. Despite severe repression, this group multiplied quickly. They created the largest population of Jews in any place and time in history, forming the largest percentage of the local population anywhere since the Jews had lost their own homeland and went into diaspora (70 C.E.). The heaviest concentration made up 10 percent of the population of Poland in 1939. At that point the Nazis systematically gathered and annihilated six million European Jews, leaving the United States as the main center of Eastern European Jewish life, rivaled in cultural energy only after 1948 by the newly revived Jewish homeland in the State of Israel, which was hostile to Yiddish culture for at least its first three decades. In the USSR, anti-Semitism went into periodic spasms under Stalin, keeping ethnic and religious identification subdued and sometimes suppressed until post-Soviet times, in the 1990s.

The eastern Ashkenazim who developed klezmer had evolved a fairly unified culture that covered a huge stretch of central, eastern, and southeastern Europe, from the Baltic Sea south to the borders of the Ottoman Empire in Turkish-occupied European lands and east toward the steppes bordering Central Asia. Their music was strongly affected by all the creative currents of the many surrounding peoples ("co-territorial" in Jewish studies terms), and it circulated through a network of traveling Jews. It is very easy to carry melodies as you travel to trade or to visit relatives, and musicians on the move did their part to cross-pollinate cultures. Also political shifts meant that large numbers of Jews moved, or were pushed, from more repressive to less restrictive regions, or migrated from depressed to more prosperous areas, accelerating cultural flow. Musical formats filtered into the klezmer world strongly from a culture nexus in southeastern Europe, where Turkish, Greek, Moldavian, Rumanian, Ukrainian, Armenian, and other cultures met. Certain genres became beloved of the Jews, probably largely for aesthetic reasons, although we have no real way of knowing why the Rumanian *doina*, for example, was carried by klezmorim from the southeast towards the north. Simultaneously, many genres and instruments the klezmorim had brought from the west in earlier migrations remained, while others were enhanced by the prestige of modern Western culture. By the late nineteenth century, with the coming of railroads and industrialization, cultural flow could only accelerate as Jews moved from the country to the city and as they set up diasporic circuits created by the huge emigration spurred by czarist policies. To date, only one serious scholarly article details the musical consequences of this cultural background (Feldman 1994/2000).

Particularly crucial to understanding European klezmer is this: while klezmorim were somewhat separated from mainstream Jewish community life, being understood as a group apart (someone even say a semi-caste), their music reflected and even helped foster the strong integration of Ashkenazic culture across all sorts of internal fault lines. Especially in the nineteenth century, the eastern Ashkenazim split into ideological camps over issues of modernization, assimilation, and types of religious affiliation, but they shared a certain aesthetic outlook when it came to musicmaking. The paraliturgical tunes heard around the dinner table on Friday night at the outset of the Sabbath (songs called *zmires*), the melodies mothers used to rock children to sleep, the love songs of young women, the highly ornamented and powerful prayer settings of the cantor in the synagogue—these and other components of the music culture were interwoven, stitched into a fabric of feeling that included those threads, principally wedding music, that belonged to the klezmer. Commentators like to say that Hasidic or cantorial melodies "influenced" klezmer, but I prefer to think of styles as strands of the same musical tapestry, woven by a shared aesthetic. It was a very colorful piece of work, since so many shades were available from the surrounding musics, and it kept changing as time made new yarns available.

That process expanded in recent decades, starting with the emigration of the culture and the musicians to other shores, especially the United States. There a freewheeling music system and a highly developed machinery of popular culture production made possible both the evolution and, eventually, the sidelining of klezmer, but always left a space for re-creation, reevaluation, revitalization, and the other "re-" terms that we reach for when trying to describe how klezmer has become so popular again, not just among Jewish Americans but accross the Atlantic. For an elegant summary of the "revival" question in the American context, Barbara Kirshenblatt-Gimblett's "Sounds of Sensibility" (1998b/2000) is required reading. Things move so quickly that this book, with its grounding in the 1980s and 1990s, can only suggest the scope of an important moment and what it means to the study of contemporary musics; the cutoff date is early 1999.

One more caution: in what follows, I will stay focused on the evolution of the instrumental music tradition, but doing so imposes a strain on the narrative. In a complicated way, eastern European vocal and instrumental music shared and exchanged ideas in daily life, but also on the stage, in the recording studio, and at the catering hall. The social distinctions between instrumentalists and vocalists have been variable, as has been their musical embodiment. A complete account of the parallel lives of these two expressive domains would immeasurably enrich our sense of "Yiddish culture" but cannot be included within these covers. "Klezmer" over the last two decades has always included both spheres in ever-surprising combinations and permutations that draw on colorful repertoires that might once have seemed incompatible. This is true in other social parameters as well, such as gender. The emergence of the all-female band, from the early revival Klezmeydlekh to the recent Mikveh, shows how inseparable the evolution of klezmer is from ongoing trends in Jewish-American culture.

Turning to the wider picture of American music studies, klezmer can help enrich the discourse of a field that, until very recently, was primarily understood as an interaction of "white" and "black" cultures, proceeding in predictable directions (whites co-opting black traditions), with the "immigrants" and the "regional" styles mostly onlookers to the main game, adding splashes of local color and ethnic pride. This model seems antique now, particularly with the lively participation of newer groups in the mix and a greater recognition of the interactivity of American life (see Slobin 1998). Klezmer is a typical hybrid system combining the diasporic with a number of sources from the dominant culture in a unique way that resonates for both "ethnic" insiders and larger audiences that pick up on its energy and distinctive sound. I have termed such musical domains "micromusics" and have suggested that they exist not as encapsulated but rather as interactive units within the larger music world of a multicultural, multimusical society like the United States. What I have termed the "superculture," the overarching commercial and official culture that all Americans know and take for granted, does not stand above and apart as a self-contained powerhouse, but rather notices, takes account of, and is often shaped by the microsystems over which it exercises hegemony (see Slobin 2000a for a detailed account of these processes).

For ethnomusicology as a whole, klezmer's profile demands attention in a number of ways. It is a transatlantic, "first-world" music that, unlike many other fast-developing systems, does not come from or spill over to the Asian, African, and Latin American/Caribbean zones of hot musical action and commodification. Also, while the diasporic nature of klezmer seems clear, its presumed homeland is felt more as an absence than as a presence. In fact, the "diaspora" (the United States) has become the music's homeland in many ways. So while klezmer "should" be understood as European—and in some ways is—it is mainly an American development and is perceived that way in Europe and even in Israel. For these and other reasons that unfold in this book, the time seems ripe to take a serious look at the klezmer world, to track the fiddlers who are ever more actively on the move.

2

Klezmer as a Heritage Music

Today's transnational, transcultural musical system offers players and consumers a huge array of large and small musics. Some are broadcast like seeds by an aggressive industry waiting for things to sprout and grow. Others emerge from collectives interested in raising their visibility, like onlookers in a crowd sitting on each other's shoulders. Still other musical systems remain largely underground in cultural burrows, emerging briefly for business and to watch out for predators.

No matter what its origins and mode of operation, every small musical system overlaps many comparable systems. In the United States this process of overlap is part of a deeply rooted habit of intertwining, in a country of immigrants and migrants. In huge movements that periodically form great waves, populations arrive from outside while insiders break up camp and move from one region to another in search of work. The history of the country becomes a list of such resettlements: the opening of the West, the conquest and settlement of the Southwest after 1848, the Ellis Island–era immigration through the early 1920s, the great African-American and Southern white migrations from south to north from the 1920s to 1940s, the post–World War II shift from the north and central states to the South and West, and the most recent influx of new groups from Asia, the Caribbean, and Latin America, producing the highest percentage in 80 years of foreign-born residents in New York and a "white" minority in California (down to 21% in San Francisco). These and many other extraordinary transitions are actually ordinary in the United States. Two main outcomes stay constant, for music: the continual building and rebuilding of a dominant system that unifies this vast and varied population, the "superculture," and the ongoing grappling with that consensus culture by small groups, "micromusics," including their need to set themselves off from it (Slobin 2000a).

11

In Europe, the modern states of the European Union find themselves in a similar state of rapid transformation, but they have been slow to adjust. The old version featured a strong center that weakened regional diversity, some long-running "minorities" (e.g., Finns in Sweden), and colonial satellites. Today the centers have declined in importance, regions have strengthened, migrants have become highly visible, and power over ex-colonies has drastically diminished. Musically, this condition results in more internal variety and greater penetration of transnational interests.

The current musical system offers a broad array of micromusics. They overlap in their structure and the ways they operate in the larger society, driven by two social forces:

Outside pigeonholing. In modern liberal democracies, states and corporations are the components of the superculture. Both have a strong interest in categories, whether for representation or target marketing. These two power brokers also overlap. Governments look at the same statistics as companies do when deciding what social units exist and how those groupings should be handled. Both also respond to the pressures that arise from the second force:

Inner needs. Groups that are counted and categorized concede the way they're defined by outsiders, seeing themselves as both "minorities," "ethnic groups," "nations," and as consumer collectives. In response, they make demands for representation, in terms of either political visibility or economic viability. They use whatever means they have: grant proposals, voting blocs, boycotts, or just the daily choices that add up to the very statistical profiles used by outsiders. But they can also react by closing in, by building ethnic boundaries that are hard for outsiders to cross or to decipher.

At present one of the main points of agreement between insiders and outsiders is the assertion of "heritage" blocs. One convenient method of lining up units for counting assumes a common connection for a particular demographic slice of the population. For example, students studying their home language at college are now called "heritage speakers." I cannot go into the extensive literature and shifting trends that make the heritage move so popular these days but I do need to take the time to connect "heritage" to music, that form of expressive culture that is (along with food) the most common way of defining group boundaries.

"Heritage" replaces older terms perhaps now thought of as problematic. A prominent victim is the word "traditional." A sentence from the work of Barbara Kirshenblatt-Gimblett, an authoritative voice in the discussion, illustrates this trend: "I use the term 'heritage music' to distinguish between music that is part and parcel of a way of life [here is where we miss the word "traditional"] and music that has been singled out for preservation, protection, enshrinement, and revival—in a word, heritage music" (Kirshenblatt-Gimblett 1998b/2000:52)

"Heritage" has become a convenient umbrella term. The interests of business, state, and insiders might converge here on a loosely defined concept that can be positively interpreted in a noncontroversial way and that can be assumed to be part of everyone's lives. The most succinct definition of the new term comes, again, from Kirshenblatt-Gimblett: "While it looks old, heritage is actually something new. Heritage is a mode of cultural production in the present that has recourse to the past" (Kirshenblatt-Gimblett 1998a:7). Once unmoored from its original straightforward meaning of "that which has been or may be inherited" (*Shorter Oxford English Dictionary*), the word floats free over ever greener semantic fields. A recent study of tourism never defines "heritage," but explains its importance in packaging people and sites for international consumption. Heritage, the authors assure us, is "the life blood" of tourism today, and "the imagery of heritage, sui generis escapist, has been maneuvered into such a position in our lives that from its treacly grasp there is little chance of escape" (Boniface and Fowler 1993:xi–xii).

Boniface and Fowler's ironic, if not cynical, stance reveals a great deal about how heritage acts as a chip in today's cultural gamesmanship. If this is the life blood of tourism, a defining moment of intergroup contact, we have moved miles beyond "tradition and modernity," or "continuity and change" the older approaches of anthropology and sociology. The people who display their "heritage" move into this new public arena of self-definition for purposes ranging from the psychological to the economic. Boniface and Fowler talk about "an increasingly wide range of culturally differentiated people visiting heritage through armchair travel—and indeed while eating and shopping" (ibid.:i). If tourism in fact does include watching commercials and eating out, then heritage really is an accepted form of cultural currency. These authors, then, agree with Kirshenblatt-Gimblett that heritage is the emerging word of choice for identification through presumed historical connection, even the most attenuated or stereotyped. Politically, heritage helps people to avoid sensitive terms like ethnicity or minority, which overlap it. Heritage even transcends the national when it is enlisted into such transnational projects as the UNESCO list of sites to be universally admired, preserved, and visited. And a company in my hometown is called Heritage Lawns, showing that the term offers an instant patina to brush on to any mundane category.

Once put into play, heritage helps crystalize the attitudes and actions of cultural tourists who find it ever easier to dip into unfamiliar lifestyles. The potential of record store browsers and festivalgoers has never been so fully tapped as it is today, with channel-surfing and Internet browsing. The late 1990s have brought new versions of heritage that do not even require getting up from your couch, most flashily the *Riverdance* and *Lord of the Dance* Irish spectaculars. Surpassing all previous ethnic presentations, this type of heritage product can be franchised from CDs to videos to large-scale stage performances, stopping just short of tie-in items at McDonalds.

Heritage musics share many structural similarities. As distinctive and historic as klezmer might be, it evolves within a network of micromusics. If we imagine musics as cultural spheres, they might be sharply defined at their cores, but their perimeters run into neighboring spheres that share some motivations, social placement, or even sonic materials. Before describing the klezmer center, I need to present a typology of heritage musics, since they seem to present themselves in clusters—constellations—rather than as single stars in our current musical galaxy. Klezmer's overlaps and its uniqueness will stand out all the more sharply after an overview of the neighboring orbits.

National

The term "nation" is used here in two senses: (1) the nation-state implied by "national dance troupe," usually a blend of selected "traditional" styles of performance; (2) the recent European trend to identify a set of named subcultures as official nations. For example, Austria now has six such nations (*Volksgruppen*) defined as long-resident distinctive groups. They are now arbitrarily and permanently demarcated as being outside the mainstream. This sense of nation tends to replace "minority" politically.

Much of this current cultural classification carries on an older romantic nationalism, which blossomed from the late eighteenth century through World War II and spawned countless folk song collections. Ideas about what is national can transcend eras, as in the case of the Hungarian revivalist movement (Frigyesi 1996), which started in presocialist times, flourished in the late socialist state (the *tanchaz* folk music club), and has morphed into newer postsocialist versions. For Hungarians, the existence of Transylvania, a Hungarian ethnic region across the border in Romania, continues to feed the need for a national narrative of authenticity.

In Poland, activists like Jan Pruszynski have recently translated the *tanchaz* for a society that is not sure what heritage means after decades of convulsive military and political nightmares. Now a largely monoethnic country like Austria, Poland has designated very small internal nations, like the Lithuanians, so their heritage can be recognized. Official acceptance as a Western country through induction into NATO will produce more pressure on Poland to move toward the new West European model: recognition of regionalism/multiculturalism (official internal difference) on the one hand and redefinition of national identity on the other.

For Hungarian and Polish folklore activists, or, to take a frightening case, the chauvinistic upholders of *izvorna* ("wellspring") forms of expression in former Yugoslavia, the idea of national heritage musics still relies heavily on peasantry. This idealized construct has survived industrialization and the arrival of a postpeasant society in a postindustrial age. The perfume of peasantry lingers long after the leading lady of romanticism has made her exit from the scene of history. In short, there will always be "national" musics, whether understood as overarching identity forms or as expressions of small-group identity within complex societies. Even Guatemala has now voted to consider itself multiethnic, showing this trend has a long future around the world.

Exotic

This notion of heritage music lies at the opposite end of the social spectrum from the national. Equally old, the exotic offers a colorful counterpart to the homespun. The two main types of exotic have been the "primitive" and the "oriental." These words resonated differently for Europeans, with their colonial connections, than for Americans, with their internal traumas of slavery and the near-extinction of indigenous peoples. The mainstream often expresses its desire for the Other, whether oriental or primitive, as the invigorator, the enlivener of pale peoples.

The end of colonialism and the influx of "foreigners" in Europe coincided with the shift of rhetoric about otherness in the United States in the post–civil rights era. Exotic musics now fall tamely into place as just another version of heritage in the multiculturalism that has supplanted nationalism. The exotic can now simply equal "someone else's heritage." It is perfectly possible to ignore the exotic, as a survey of Danish teenagers (Fock 1997) has shown. These high school students happily embrace the commercial world beat sounds of African and Latin drumming offered by the transnational media, but they show no interest in the musical styles connected to immigrant neighbors. Exposure to middle Eastern and East Asian musics through school programs does not produce acceptance of strange sounds. It seems there are two kinds of exotic: the local "ethnic" and the faraway. An exotic music can move from one column to the other in a very short time. In Britain the ascendance of South Asian-based pop from the exotic margins to the top of the national charts offers a striking example. Whereas the first wave of South Asian musicians operated under a "black" British umbrella, the current top-selling artists deny that their music is "heritage," preferring to inherit the mantle of pop stardom.

Faraway exotics can also become deeply entrenched in the mainstream mind. The passion for Native American culture was so prevalent that in Germany, becoming an "Indian" was part of growing up for many boys. Today Native Americans go to Europe on different terms from when they appeared as colorful but inarticulate exotics. As the *New York Times* notes: "today's Buffalo Bills are more likely to be anthropologists, historical guardians or savvy artists. Many Indian performing artists have begun to establish European contacts . . . but others have an agent handle details of museum exhibitions, folk festivals, fund-raising, and transportation of sacred objects" (May 26, 1998). The Indians themselves say "people there think we must be wearing moccasins, but a lot of us have Nikes." Heritage exoticism can just be a form of portable tourism.

Traditional uses of the exotic as musical source material have been pushed beyond the usual limits by the accelerated distribution of world music since the 1980s, a trend pushed by the major recording companies. In a radio interview (KUSP, June 9, 1998), the singer of the San Francisco band Stella Mara explained that not only does she sing in many different languages she doesn't understand, but she now writes songs in English and then has them translated into the language that "feels right" for the song. This creative process lays bare the implicit control that musicians of a dominant culture exercise over the cultural raw materials of resource-rich exotics.

The local exotic as a subtype exerts a powerful charm for some main-streamers. An extensive study of West Berlin's musical subcultures (Brandes et al. 1986), done just before German reunification, focused on 85 groups falling into three implicit headings: music of Germans from other regions, music of non-Germans played by those people themselves, and performing groups of non-German musics with a heavy German presence. There is a social shimmer arising from all this interaction, making it not easy to sort out recognizable types, but this much is clear: individually and collectively, some Germans feel they should—or would love to—support or even play the local exotic musics of their city. Social scripts being subject to rewriting, the sudden termination in the mid-1990s of Berlin's municipal funding for the musical Other tells a great deal about the fragility of representation.

The protected space of the American university supports different varieties of exoticism. First introduced as part of a 1950s academic experiment in what UCLA's Mantle Hood called "bimusicality," the idea of offering various shades of otherness for undergraduate credit became completely routine. Starting with orientalism—Indian music and the Javanese gamelan orchestra—and extending to the "primitive" styles of Africa, now re-valued as rhythmic and ethnic enrichment, ethnomusicology's domestication of the exotic extended to African-American representation around 1970. Logically following domestic political agendas, the trend has since broadened to include Latin America both as domestic and foreign exotic (e.g., Chicano music at UCLA, Andean music in Illinois), among other academically acceptable "nonwestern" possibilities. These notions of otherness coincided with commercial versions when college campuses became the major venues for "world music" tours. A generation earlier, the internal American exotic—the rural folk musician—had depended heavily on academic legitimization and concert dates. Klezmer became part of this college experimentation as early as 1978, when Hankus Netsky started the first academic class at the New England Conservatory under the "third-stream" rubric, but klezmer still has not spread much as a course offering, perhaps because of its ambiguous status within the exotic-to-heritage spectrum.

Space does not allow for a well-considered mapping of the dense, uncharted forests of symbols that exotic musics create in the Euro-American mind. Only recently have studies like the Berlin project begun to sketch out the boundaries of the problem. One highly relevant recent study by Mirjana Laušević looks closely at Americans who fervently and deeply take up the cause of Balkan music and dance. Much of what she describes probably holds true for European "Balkanites" as well. A striking section of Laušević's study details various individuals' passionate response to an alien music. For example, Tamar says, "It was really visceral, it was something at the gut level, the first time I heard *chlgija*. Something just hit me in my soul and I thought: I am going to go to Macedonia." Stewart says, "I felt it had power over me. It's a connection to universality, to inner harmony" (Laušević 1998:359–60). These two comments alone offer rich material for understanding the pull of an exotic heritage music. Tamar immediately ties her "gut" experience to a faraway but very concrete place—Macedonia—to which she now must make a pilgrimage. Stewart finds that the exotic sounds move him toward a more cosmic space which, for some Balkanites, evokes the New Age fascination with the influence of past lives. Such a range of responses to the exotic implies that heritage is somewhat secondary to the outsider. The lightning–strike reaction comes entirely from within the individual's psyche, rather than being conditioned by membership in, or long familiarity with, unaccustomed music communities. No harsh social realities intrude on the fantasy world of the devotees of the Balkan exotic, a particularly striking reaction in the case of such a turbulent and politically problematic region.

The exotic can be much more powerful than the national or the diasporic (the next section), since an imaginary connection that fuels the fires of passion can even drive a person to lifelong commitment.

Diasporic

This is an ancient type of heritage music that has only recently been identified officially and academically (see Slobin 1994 for a survey). The term "diasporic" describes musics belonging to a minority population away from home, living in a multigroup society abroad. The homeland may have little connection to the development of a heritage music. A prominent example in the United States is the Polish-American polka, which broke through the visibility ceiling forcefully enough to gain a Grammy Award category. That achievement underscores the Americanness of the music, which is unknown in Poland. At the other end of the spectrum lie styles that are constantly being invented and refined both in the host country and in the homeland as part of the cyclical movement of bands and audiences, as is often the case with Caribbean styles (Averill 1994). In between lies a whole range of diasporic music-making representing tighter or looser ties to the homeland. Many micromusics shift according to the contingencies of history, such as the sudden independence of the Baltic states in 1991 (Estonia, Latvia, Lithuania), which shifted allegiances and expectations on both sides of the diaspora, with musical results.

In Europe much of the activity in the West Berlin study was exotic to Germans but diasporic to the music communities described, such as Kurds and Turks. The complexity of this type of situation has been very well described for Sweden (Hammarlund 1994, Ronstrom 1992), the first European country where ethnomusicologists took the notion of diaspora seriously. The geographic compactness of Europe allows for multiple, closely timed interchanges between a diasporic population and its home. Even in the 1980s a Yugoslav musician could simply drive to Germany for work and return home quickly, playing for other Yugoslavs who were bi- or multilocal, such as the Bosnian musician Mensur Hatić profiled in the textbook *Worlds of Music* (Slobin 1996).

How much of this music qualifies as "diasporic" is less than clear, since the word is a recently coined adjective form of an old noun. The closer you look, the more ambiguous any instance becomes. For example, does the fact that Mensur Hatić now lives in Detroit make him diasporic when there is no Yugoslav homeland he can relate to? He comes from Brčko, a town on the Serbian edge of Bosnia, which at the turn of the millennium remains a place with an indeterminate fate. For the Americans who come to Hatić's workshops, his homeland is something of a dreamland, as we've seen. To them, he certainly figures as an exotic more than a diasporic musician. But these American cultural explorers have internalized their version of a Balkan way of life so thoroughly, in terms of cooking and household decoration, that exotic hardly qualifies the way it might for a college audience listening for the first time to the astonishing sounds of Tuvan throat singers from Siberia.

Postdiasporic/rediasporic

There are groups whose heritage work seems insufficiently described by "diasporic." For Jewish Americans, African Americans, and Latinos, the homeland connection seems extraordinarily complex. I will turn to the Jewish case below. For African Americans, the long displacement from their homeland under traumatic conditions has always involved a unique process of imagination and reconnection. Once mostly mythic, that vision is now tied to a set of postcolonial African nation-states and is only slowly settling into a pattern of mutual recognition and affiliation (Ebron 1998). The concept of "African diaspora" itself is rather recent in African-American thinking but has now become completely accepted. The multiple base of the diaspora—North America, the Caribbean, South America—makes the situation even more complicated.

For Latinos, ever more frequently projected as America's largest "minority heritage group," things are not much simpler. The term "Latinos" (and its alternate, Hispanics) blankets peoples whose history and sense of homeland differ enormously. This group is coalescing around cable television networks largely driven by music and mass entertainment. The effects of a vast commercial process blur the question of diaspora even more than usual, since markets are doing much of the work of projecting a common Latino musical heritage. Meanwhile, with dual citizenship for Mexican Americans becoming a reality, the contiguous populations of the United States and Mexico continue to redefine notions of diaspora, homeland, and heritage in ways that include innovative musical patterns.

Traditional transnational

Rounding out types of heritage music scenes, one unavoidable category remains: "traditional" musics picked up by the entertainment industry over the last hundred years and scattered around the world systematically. From the very start, record companies invented group-specific labels to sell musical items, performers, and styles, intending to target niche markets. Over time, layer upon musical layer of technologically enhanced sound piled up in a stratigraphy of sentiment. Marketed originally to local populations, these musics spread quickly and insinuated themselves into the sensibilities of people in widely separate regions. Histories of some of these systems exist, but rarely do researchers approach them transnationally. There are few specialized studies and no unified approach to the global spread of the American ragtime and blues, the Hawaiian craze, the passion for tango (Savigliano 1995 makes a start here), the various Irish/Celtic styles, the folk song revival of the 1950s, or reggae and hip-hop in the 1980s, although these and other similarly magnetic forms have helped to homogenize human musical experience. All these musical tributaries flow into a mainstream that changes other forms of heritage musics into backwaters, local whirlpools, and eddies that might be suitable largely for purposes of tourism.

The commercial recording industry keeps scanning scenes for possible marketable units, ranging from whole traditions through isolated instruments. The result is events like the penny whistle boom of 1998, which Jon Pareles eloquently describes as typical:

A sweet sound is on the verge of curdling, and it is time to save it from overexposure. This happens to instruments, and it's not a pretty process. It happened to the sitar . . . to the Cajun accordion and to panpipes. . . . Rousted from their ethnic enclaves, the instruments' masters revel in their new-found prominence. Then, too late, they realize that they're only the flavor of the moment, and the moment never lasts. (*New York Times*, April 8, 1998)

Pareles details the whole cycle of an instrument's fame, from obscurity, popularization, and installation as a preset on a keyboard through revival twenty years later as "simple nostalgia or forgiven kitsch." All his examples are "ethnic" in origin.

A question Pareles does not raise is whether these popular culture balloons remain tethered to the ground of a heritage as they float into full visibility. When does the penny whistle stop being Celtic? How many of the listening billions still relate the basic form of the blues, or even the schematics of rapping, to African-American inspiration? How often does Argentina come to mind among the devoted tangophiles of Finland? Like the emerging euro, musics can spiral beyond individual origins to act as a common, neutral currency. Yet even the euro, by its very name, denominates some sort of homeland, albeit a manufactured metaspace. It does seem that reggae remains tied to Caribbeanism, while the meteoric 1980s dance craze called lambada was linked through music videos to a more generalized Latin tropicalism. Hawaii has remained pretty steady in its imaginative rooting over the decades. It is useless to generalize about the fate of widespread musical types, but it is helpful to think through the knotty issues raised by this type of transnational heritage music.

IN THE BIG PICTURE, we see overlaps of overlays. National subtends the diasporic, for without a historical grounding of peoplehood, the concept of diaspora loses most of its force. The traditional transnational musics draw heavily on diasporic creativity, very pointedly in the case of African-American styles as part of cross-Africana interaction such as reggae's skillful blending of African-American components and hip-hop's inspiration from Jamaican techniques. The idea of the exotic was greatly magnified by the spread of commercial recordings, which made faraway sounds part of everyday life in many corners of the world. In this context, mainstream Western music itself becomes exotic, than national as received by non-Western peoples like the Chinese. To keep multiplying overlaps would be tedious. The point is that they clarify points of intersection, but also freestanding cores. At its center, each of the types discussed here retains a kernel of distinctiveness that informs us about the nature of micromusical systems as a whole.

WE CAN NOW TURN TO KLEZMER, positioning its profile on the set of overlaps just suggested, category by category:

National

It is perhaps in this category that klezmer stands apart most clearly. Again, comparison with the Irish situation makes things clear. A *New York Times* article (Peter Applebome, June 8, 1998) on the late-1990s Irish music boom is titled "Rooted in Ireland's soil, but growing everywhere." The article quotes Steve Berlin of Los Lobos, the California Mexican band: "There's a specific and almost palpable similarity between Irish culture and Mexican culture." Applebome attributes the strength of the trend to two factors. First he cites the "remarkably ecumenical quality of Irish culture [which] seems to travel so well and include so much far-flung music amicably under the same tent." This factor does suggest an overlap with klezmer's placement, but the writer goes onto set up a clearer boundary, the idea that "Ireland, for better or worse, is finally becoming integrated into the rest of the world." This image of a confident, solidly based national music system reaching out to and being embraced by a panoply of performers and impresarios suggests a dimension of heritage that is simply not available to klezmer.

Klezmer partakes of the national in a distinctive, if not unique fashion. Instead of a homeland as the anchor, some reference to "Jewishness" pervades the production and reception of this music. The word *yiddishkayt*, a Yiddish word for the essential quality of homespun Jewishness, often appears in the discourse around klezmer. But the nature of Jewishness has been furiously debated over the centuries, accelerating in the twentieth century to the point of obsession. Jews seeking national expression might well turn to klezmer at critical ritual points such as life-cycle events (weddings, bar mitzvahs) or communal celebrations of holidays. Record companies or world music impresarios looking for token representation of the Jewish might well notice klezmer. Even this approach is not straightforward; looking for klezmer albums in record stores can be time-consuming. If there is not a catch-all Jewish bin, often the music appears in a Middle Eastern section alongside Israeli, Arabic, and Turkish music, but there are many other possibilities, including a spot between folk and country, an intriguing slot that suggests deep Americanness rather than a "national" identity.

Sometimes tourism seems to offer a local intersection between klezmer and the national. In Budapest the brochure for "klezmer" handed out on the street has the same format as the flyer for "folklore," suggesting a direct parallel between the Hungarian State Folk Ensemble and the Budapester Klezmer Band, including the identical daily schedule of events and information in six languages. The resemblance peters out when you read the fine print describing the twin heritage projects. For the Hungarian ensemble's tunes and dances, we learn that "some of them were collected in isolated villages and date back hundreds of years." The narrative for "Cultural and Musical Jewish Heritage of Budapest" does begin (inaccurately) with "the biggest Jewish population in Eastern Europe lived always in Budapest," suggesting authenticity, but then it continues this way: "the Budapester Klezmer Band was formed in the spring of 1990 as an effect of the revival of the American klezmer music." We have run straight into the ironies and ambiguities of modern klezmer. Stylings developed in the United States are almost desperately thrown into the cultural chasm caused by the Holocaust. The sense of the local Jewish band being "national" is redirected toward a feeling for the diasporic. Ultimately the brochure suggests that the central European roots of klezmer can only be imported from the United States and transplanted back to their area of origin.

The Budapest example suggests that klezmer as the national remains an ambiguous and multifaceted concept in Europe. Multiple versions include: (1) the Jews as an ancient, pre-European nation; (2) the Jews as a pre-World War II nation within older national boundaries (strong in Central Europe); (3) the Jews as the victimized nation; (4) the Jews as the phantom nation, needing representation but nearly absent (again strong in Central Europe, particularly Poland) (5) the Jews as a transnational nation (at worst, an international conspiracy), especially including the United States; (6) the Jews as a multinational nation, including Israel; and (7) the Jews as a representative multicultural nation in the new European order. These and their variants place any discussion of klezmer way off the overlap map. In the United States the perplexities about the Jews take different forms, with few correlations with the European situation save for (1) the multicultural view, and (2) the ancient, biblical nation concept. Further, in the American context, we find (3) the recently deracialized nation embedded within the majority "white" population, hence socially invisible; (4) the potentially victimized nation needing special treatment; (5) the politically powerful, potentially conspiratorial nation; and (6) the diasporic nation tied to the replacement homeland of Israel.

What are the consequences for klezmer of these diverse, often contradictory approaches to Jewish nationhood? The most obvious lies in an absence, the parameter that refuses to pop up: romantic nationalism. Of all the external evaluations listed here, none stresses what is "normal" for European essentialist or American apple-pie musics: sentimental nostalgia. For Europeans, this emotion never made sense for thinking about the Jews, except in relation to Zionism, the re-creation of a non-European, ancient homeland for the Jews. In the United States, thinking back to the way Jews were treated in Europe tended to preclude nostalgia. In the early 1960s *Fiddler on the Roof* finally provided a safe place for visiting the European past, a niche klezmer has inherited. In mainstream and media consciousness, the twin visions of the Holocaust and the State of Israel tend to be much more regularly embedded. So we have a nice case study of how heritage—nurtured by Broadway and sustained by the emergence of vest- and cap-wearing bands—privileges user-friendly and sentimentalized formulations of group recognition. A stereotyped imagery of the past clings to klezmer long after it has rubbed off the Jewish people as a whole.

Not surprisingly, Germany is where some of these issues of Jewish identity through music come to the fore. Here is a review from the *Berliner Tageszeitung* of the prominent band Brave Old World: "The passion and history of the Jewish people is always present when Brave Old World plays, but never overly sentimental or confronting." The critic is saying that he likes the romance of the Jewish nation's past but wants to keep it at a distance, emotionally and politically. Another journalist, from Stuttgart, is even more conflicted: "Here in Germany we'd almost forgotten how multilayered and soulful music can be, and what a treasure Jewish culture can offer us . . . music that goes beyond all geographic, cultural, and emotional boundaries" (citations from Brave Old World's website, 1998). Fully endorsing the power of Jewish national identity located in klezmer, this critic then wants to relocate that intensity somewhere "beyond all boundaries," presumably to avoid having to deal with the German history attached to Jewish nationhood. To round out this short reference to the complexity of European response to klezmer, here is the *Nieuwe Rotterdamse Courant:* "Their instrumental pieces . . . sound flowing and light, the vocals and recitations are powerful and convincing, and they don't shy away from drama and pathos," as if it those elemental emotions were really harmful to the band's success. I would argue that it is exactly the national component of klezmer that this writer also wants the band to rein in, or at least to balance carefully with "flowing and light" melodies.

In the North American scene the national is easier to assimilate to klezmer. It simply is a well-known musical branch of the Jewish identity tree. It would be tedious to cite the number of album liner notes that talk about klezmer in some essentialist way (see Slobin 1988 for this approach on early neo-klezmer album covers). Yet it would be just as lengthy to list the number of times bands seek to move beyond that national narrative of European origins and American rootings to stress that they have something else to offer. Returning to reviews of Brave Old World, the American blurbs differ from the European takes cited above; for example, a review in *Sing Out!* shows a certain weariness: "These men have been every-klezmer-where. They've played every tune and sung every song; they're tired of everything that's usual and obvious. They're moving on. If you are bored by the basics, this is for you." Presumably the basics not only include tunes and texts, but appeal to the Jewish national nature of klezmer music. The band itself feels this way, as their spokesman Alan Bern says in the liner notes for their album *Blood Oranges* (1997): "For us, this recording is a liberation from endless debates about authenticity, history, and social significance, and an affirmation of music which simply celebrates its own freedom: 'New Jewish Music.'" Brave Old World, then, wants to be Jewish but unencumbered, truly a hopeful idea of nationhood in the face of Jewish history.

The "downtown" New York experimentation of composer John Zorn's circle seems further removed from traditional *yiddishkayt* than Brave Old World. Zorn, once a standard-bearer of cosmopolitan avant-gardism in the 1970s, now also supports a vision of national innovation through his record label Tzadik, with its Radical Jewish Culture logo, and his own band Masada. A word like *tzadik*, traditionally reserved for a great sage, or Masada, site of the ancient Israelites' last stand against the Roman army, implicates Zorn in a deep nationalism that the work of his circle belies. Ranging from sixties jazz styles through avant-garde experimentation, Radical Jewish Culture seems more a commentary on the identity of New York artists than a "national" project. But when Masada plays six concerts in Taipei, perhaps the audience abstracts a national project from the Ornette Coleman–style arrangements.

More traditionally, mainstream klezmer bands create an American-based Jewish national narrative by referencing the klezmer–jazz interface of the early twentieth century, which they can rehearse or update. This urge began even in the earliest neo-klezmer albums, strikingly on the first release of the seminal Klezmer Conservatory Band (1980), for which band-leader Hankus Netsky chose to include "Yidishe Blues," a 1918 experiment by Lt. Joseph Frankel. The piece blends a ragtime sensibility in instrumentation and syncopation with a klezmer melodic line. By insisting on including the rank "Lt.," Frankel was already signaling an American-ness for the Jewish nation. Suitably, Frankel was a band officer in both the Russian and American armies, a fact that reveals the futility of trying to anchor any specific Jewish national identity in the twentieth century. Even as Frankel was evolving a hyphenated Jewish-American musical identity, other bandleaders were still using "national" to reference the European side, as in Abe Schwartz's "National Hora" (discussed later). Updating Frankel's work of hybridization has become basic to recent klezmer bands, like the New Orleans Klezmer All-Stars, or even newer regional experimentalists like Schloinke, whose points of reference are much more American than European. Schloinke's idea of the national includes playing the theme from the television cartoon *Underdog* as a klezmer tune.

Finally, at the far end of conservatism, Andy Statman, a veteran of the secular 1970s klezmer revival, has moved toward the spiritual side of nationhood, much stressed throughout Jewish-American culture in the late 1990s, a long way from his earlier "shtetl" authenticity style of the late 1970s. Riffing on old Hasidic tunes with jazz-based sidemen, he stresses the sacred nature of the music and distances himself from the very word "klezmer." Also in the mid-1990s he released an album with bluegrass/newgrass buddy David Grisman, which combines black and white photos of the European past with liner notes stressing the national identity of individualistic Jewish musicians who are returning to roots after achieving all-American stardom.

Even a short, dizzying run through klezmer identity projects should show the head-scratching quality of trying to define the "national" in the Jewish case, as opposed to, say, the Hungarian or Irish worlds. We should not be surprised. In the 200 years since modernity came to the Jewish world, neither outsiders nor insiders have agreed on the nature of the Jewish nation/race/religion/ethnic group/minority. It is even possible to identify strongly with klezmer music without associating it with Jews. One young musician I talked to in Berlin in 1997 told me someone had given her an album she really liked, with music she tried to re-create for over a year, until she looked hard enough at the liner notes to see what the Klezmatics represented, which included a Jewish identity. So perhaps overemphasis on the Jewishness of the klezmer phenomenon might in itself be a familiar trap; Jews so often assume everyone is concerned with their nationhood, and they are so often right in this assumption, that they tend to forgot it isn't always true.

Exotic

The extent to which klezmer overlaps with the exotic component of heritage musics is perhaps more straightforward than with the "national," more commonly in Europe. Since no one on that continent can really remember klezmer as a living tradition, and in almost all countries of the European Union, it was rarely if ever seen on the streets, the possibility of perceiving it as at least slightly exotic is indeed available. Here whatever romantic tinge still lingers about the Jewish past overlaps with the exotic, the past being seductive—if you want it to be.

Since the French usually do want the past and the faraway to seduce them, a look at liner notes might be revealing, as in the case of one mid-1990s album. The band's name itself makes a bold statement: Orient Express Moving Shnorers. The romance of travel in the old days—Orient Express—is combined with an English and a Yiddish word to place the whole title firmly outside the French orbit. Their album is in a series called "Transes européenes" (European trances), and it is annotated this way: "what balms, what unguents can revive the pure marvel which was the intense life of populations decimated today?" and it continues by citing the fiddler on the roof and an entire panoply of songs and dances that surge out of the millennia. While this rhetoric might seem limited to the romantic past, the band's basic credo (in English) describes them as "artists whose creative approach integrates the existence of cultures other than their own . . . [echoing] the world's multiple musical resonances." In other words, the past really is another country, and it can live again in our days through the intervention of some Jews who still remember, "inheritors of the klezmer on the soil of France." A typically French move is made to equate the resident ethnic with the exotic.

Despite this reassuring solidarity, the European Jew as exotic can only be tied to the lost Jew of the past, since present-day Jews are all too familiar citizens as well as bones of contention in the body politic of many European countries. Klezmer thus is set off from the normal faraway musics, tinged by the romantic allure of travel. As local exotics, klezmer musicians also do not fit well into the European context, since the whole klezmer phenomenon tends to be imported from the United States. So what makes klezmer exceptional is the way it offers Europeans a vision of Americans as representing a romantic, faraway musical tradition. Being more typically associated with mainstream American mythology—country/western,

Native American, African-American—klezmer breaks new ground in the exotic category. The appearance of American klezmorim might resemble the current jetstreamlined forms that exotic Americana takes on when it appears in Europe. So far, klezmer bands have avoided the use of middlemen such as the Indians employ, who describe themselves as "helping Indians do business overseas," but transatlantic commerce has become a major part of making a living and projecting your talent.

Klezmer as a type of local exotic music does fill a slot in the multicultural atmosphere of today's Europe. Vienna was never a klezmer city, even when it was 20 percent Jewish before 1938, since Eastern European Jewry did not set the tone for the local modernizing, assimilating culture. Today the city is nearly 20 percent "foreign" (immigrant), with a tiny but hardy population of about 10,000 very diverse Jews. It is as a modern multicultural metropolis that Vienna experiences the *ostjüdisch* ("east Jewish," usually not a compliment) music it formerly didn't miss. There are many similarities here with Berlin, the most active European site of new Jewish music-making.

To explain "multicultural," it is useful to make a comparative move and introduce evidence about "black" music in Vienna. Writing in an anthology on musical "diversity" (Hemetek 1996), Filip Lamasisi, a musician and ethnomusicologist from Papua New Guinea, describes the history of a band he formed with a Nigerian immigrant:

> After our inaugural gig at a cultural function in one of the cultural centers in Vienna, we were able to extend our appointments further to night clubs, private functions including birthday parties and wedding ceremonies. . . . Gradually we felt a need to generate more sound . . . and this was achieved as an Austrian friend and keyboarder joined us to form a Trio.
>
> We tried to bring to public awareness, i.e., the audience, some basic musical elements that perhaps were foreign to them, while at the same time creating an entertainment (tropical) atmosphere, which the music presumably represented and reflected. . . . In general, the experiences we gained in our encounters, both during performance and beyond, encompassed positive and negative ones. (Lamasisi 1996:95)

One of the principal performers of Jewish music in Vienna is Leon Pollak, an immigrant from Poland via Israel. He chanced upon the klezmer path by being asked to play at a birthday party and a wedding, then branched out to small clubs and community events. He says that audience reception has been both positive and negative, since listeners are responding to musical elements that surprise them. When you ask him if

Austrian audiences understand klezmer as exotic, he says "completely." Rounding out the parallel to Lamasisi's band, the other members of Pollak's trio include a Bulgarian Roma ("gypsy") musician well versed in "eastern" sounds and an Austrian bass player fluent in Viennese and theater music styles.

While there are considerable overlaps in the accounts of these two "ethnic" bandleaders from Vienna, the differences are also glaring, given the historical status of the Jews in Vienna and nonhistorical status of "blacks" as a category. An especially important difference is the Jewish community's active engagement with Pollak's work, as opposed to the basically touristic mission of the "black" band. Common to both is their positioning as heritage musics in a large metropolitan music system in a multicultural society. Lamasisi's band is constantly aware of transnational trends, of the whole range of black music (reggae and calypso) that they must integrate into their performance, music that is native to neither "black" musician. Pollak, who grew up without much Jewish music background either in Poland or Israel, has subsumed American and European klezmer archival sources into his repertoire as a way of being a comprehensive representative of his tradition. This single example of one Vienna bandleader can stand in for a wide range of micromusical moments in progress all across Europe, where klezmer musicians represent the exotic to outsiders while trying to establish a community base as insiders.

In the United States the exotic possibilities of klezmer might play a little differently, since Americans are familiar with the idea of new, colorful local or regional styles entering mainstream consciousness. After all, most of the traditional transnational musics that swept the world started in America as breakthroughs of otherness: ragtime, blues, Hawaiian, folk songs, bluegrass, cajun/zydeco. These and other old and remodeled traditions quickly become heritage musics. Ultimately they fill the need for the otherness that proves we are all "the same," a political-musical rhetoric that is only slowly infiltrating Europe. Klezmer has made an exceptional leap in upward mobility through the agency of Itzhak Perlman. With the exception of the neo-Irish dance craze, it is uncommon for Radio City Music Hall or the Kennedy Center to sell out for a minor heritage music, or for an album of that style to sell over 200,000 copies. The intersection of the old fiddling tradition with the violin virtuoso image makes an unexpected linkage that can be highly marketable in the American context. To what extent exoticism spices the stew could be determined only by some survey that is yet to be done. Certainly the lesson has not been lost on other classical virtuosi, as is shown by cellist Yo-Yo Ma's forays into American old-time music and Argentine new tango, where he was joined by violinist Gidon Kremer and pianist Daniel Bairenboim. The last two being from the same artistic and ethnic background as Perlman, it seems that exoticizing one's persona while stressing ethnic identity remains a rare choice.

Diasporic

I have already touched on the singularity of the Jewish situation, with the destruction of its home region and the creation of the State of Israel, but the issue is even more complex: East Europe was not really a homeland. That is, there was no resting place in the diaspora (Yiddish: *goles*), which was viewed as a 2,000-year exile that could be ended only with the advent of the Messiah and the ingathering of Jews in Zion. This is the sharpest break between conventional and Jewish approaches to diaspora.

In the United States in recent decades, something unique to diaspora studies has taken place: a slowly evolving but now blossoming nostalgia for diaspora. Courses in Yiddish, the diaspora language par excellence, have multiplied. The old Yiddish-language films from the time of immigrant diaspora (1910s–1930s) are constantly on the screens. The National Yiddish Book Center, located in Amherst, Massachusetts, far from Jewish population centers, started by reclaiming those orphans of history, Yiddish books, and has grown into a major cultural site. Its marketing strums steadily on the strings of remembrance. In this setting of nostalgic diasporism, klezmer has set down its strongest roots.

The Jewish diasporic music spectrum presents its own system of overlaps. In the United States there is some dovetailing of tunes and personnel between the non-Orthodox, mainstream klezmer world and the musical space of Orthodox and Hasidic Jews, despite a deep ideological gulf that divides these branches of American Jewry. In Israel, Joel Rubin found that there is also some crossover between modern klezmer music and tunes played traditionally by Hasidic communities or learned from American recordings. "Klezmer music is still an integral part of the *simkhe* [ritual celebration] context . . . and it is tied both to the Jewish religious calendar and life-cycle events as it once was in Europe. It is imbedded in a milieu where music plays an important role from early childhood on, and where the boundaries between sacred and secular are blurred" (Rubin 1998:19). This situation is also not the normal diasporic heritage context. Moshe Berlin, an Israeli clarinetist who has always played what are now called klezmer tunes for the Hasidic community's celebrations, has recently generalized his self-definition by fronting a klezmer-oriented band and saying that "klezmer music is the way a Jew plays music after the destruction of the Temple in Jerusalem," and that "Jews from other Diasporas" (East, Far East, Middle East, etc.) have their own "klezmer too" (e-mail communication to Jewish music list, February 2000).

In no case would Hasidim embrace a secular term like "heritage." Even in the United States, when I asked the head of Detroit's Hasidic community whether his people might participate in the Michigan Folklore Festival, a classic heritage event, he simply said they would have nothing to do with such *narishkayt* (foolishness).

So we are left with secularized Jews looking for a diasporic tie-in to their music-making, a process elegantly summarized by Barbara Kirshen-blatt-Gimblett (1998b). This move toward roots parallels the general drive for reaffiliation with Jewishness that has snowballed since the 1960s to become the most important trend in Jewish-American life. The klezmer repertoire is one of the handiest points of connection, since it does not require getting lost in the thickets of sacred text, and you can dance to it. But most strongly, this body of tunes is already Americanized, deeply and doubly diasporic. That is, the canonical items that must be learned by any fledgling klezmer band come from 78 RPM recordings, 90 percent of which were recorded in New York City around 1917–1932. At that time Jewish Americans did in fact carry on an intense transatlantic ethnic life that fits our usual description of diasporic. They went home to search for brides, to visit aged relatives, or to do business, and that home was another diaspora, Eastern Europe. Musicians went back and forth in search of trade, notably the entrepreneurial sacred singers known as cantors (Slobin 1989). Walter Zev Feldman (1994) has shown that the demands of the recording studio and the evolving taste of the Jewish audience pushed the core klezmer repertoire in directions congenial to the social and musical atmosphere of the United States. This meant that players emphasized specific genres and approaches even while giving the recorded pieces European names or interpoling Yiddish patter. Eventually these pressures would drive klezmer to the margins of Jewish-American musical consciousness, intensified by the creation of Israel as substitute homeland in 1948.

So for klezmer, as opposed to most heritage musics today, the diasporic is a thing of the past, or it needs to be repositioned as part of a new nostalgia. In Western Europe the American diaspora has become authentic, since it is from the United States that the concept of purely instrumental "Yiddish" dance music comes. This trend has actually created a surprising diaspora of American musicians who spend much of their time, or who even live, in places like Budapest or Berlin. Michael Alpert, a key figure in the modern klezmer movement, has recounted the deep irony and ambiguity of this situation in his liner notes to Brave Old World's album *Beyond the Pale:* "In 1993, Germany is one of the very few countries where you can make a living playing Jewish music. But for whom. . . . So play me a sweet Diaspora song, with a longing that's pure," a line from the song "Berlin 1990" that actually made it to Germany's hit charts, with this diasporic sentiment (translation from Yiddish by Alpert):

> My own heritage is ever on my mind
> Even as I traverse the bright present.
> Because if not for the wars, pogroms, slaughter
> I too would have been Europe's progeny.

Here an American, reflecting on the irony of representing Jewishness to Germans, considers the possibility of the multiple diasporas history offers the Jews, even while evoking a "sweet Diaspora song."

Since the diaspora problem is tightly tied to the definition of homeland, it is remarkably perceptive of Alpert to devote a song on the 1997 album *Blood Oranges* to this issue, trying out the full range of meanings for "homeland." In a song with that title, Alpert proposes a cluster of images that modify, extend, and deconstruct the word:

> Homeland of my oft-shed tears
> Homeland with me through the years
> Homeland drive away my fears
> Homeland far apart

Here Alpert offers a fairly nostalgic point of view, but he quickly juxtaposes it with a much more generalized semantic field for the term:

> And every one of us is each
> A homeland to ourselves

which is later exploded to:

> Homeland where my love is true.
> Homeland me and homeland you.
> Homeland Christian, Muslim, Jew,
> Homeland not at war.

If homeland can be so contested a concept, then diaspora, seemingly so obvious for the Jews, emerges as one of the subtlest of overlaps in the heritage music system. Such terms as rediasporization and postdiasporization seem much more plausible, if hard to handle.

Traditional transnational

We move to more solid ground with this overlap of the heritage music system. Klezmer was not one of the highly visible traditional transnational musics in its early recording heyday, as were the tango, ragtime, and blues. Nor was it picked up on in the 1950s–1960s surge of transnational "folk" styles that spread across the United States and Europe in waves that continued through the 1970s. The American folk revival of the Weavers did introduce Jewish material briefly, before the New Left decreed that Jewish themes were politically incorrect, but the Old Left singers chose the Palestinian settlers' songs or a couple of "folk song" items (actually of literary origin) to represent Jewishness rather than what might have been more obvious, the down-home klezmer dance tunes Pete Seeger could have reeled off on his banjo.

The later diffusion of klezmer has much in common with the way other traditional transnational styles have moved listeners to reflection and emulation through recordings and touring bands. In the United States, as the literature is beginning to show (Kirshenblatt-Gimblett 1998b/2000), and as foundational klezmer figures have always admitted, the folk revival sensibility and professional background of performers was key to the emergence of klezmer on the American scene in the 1970s. It is also the existence of the heritage music infrastructure—the festival network, the small folk labels—that first brought klezmer into European consciousness. Disparate heritage musics share a single socioeconomic profile: they are all "subcommodified." The -commodified half of the term is easy enough: All these musics depend to some extent on exchange of money, expressed through venues and recordings, as much as on aesthetic appeal. While many traditional transnational musicians have day jobs, few are willing to be completely unpaid and unrecorded. But it is the extent to which they are commodified that produces the prefix -sub. There are no major record label deals here, no arena concerts, no massive sale of T-shirts and memorabilia. By the standards of world musical commodification, klezmer is one of many heritage musics that cruise beneath the radar of full-scale entrepreneurial developers. While there are exceptions—notably the Irish marketing breakout of *Riverdance* and *Lord of the Dance* cited earlier—rewards remain small for doing the work of heritage musicianship.

No, it's mostly not for the money, but through the drive for acquiring ever more musical styles as a savvy connoisseur, jaded listener, or enthusiastic instrumentalist that these traditional transnational musics have spread across the literal and musical landscape. Traveling in Europe in 1997, I heard repeatedly that klezmer was being played simply because it was the latest version of a long-time pattern of youth musics with a roots feel. Otherwise, it's hard to imagine why there is an Italian klezmer fad. No trick of diasporic consciousness or national identification can explain Italians wanting to play and listen to klezmer. A young band I interviewed in Bologna, Dire-gelt, described the situation this way:

From time to time there is a different kind of folk music that's a trend in Italy. Twenty years ago it was folk music from south Italy, then came music from the Celtic areas of Europe; now it's the klezmer time; it's the right moment.

How many bands in Italy? A lot. Klezmer is grouped with East European; it's the thing you most hear in the ethnic situation. Every one of us has a different surrounding around klezmer music; Yiddish theater. . . . It's spreading around day after day.

These trends can have a short shelf life. According to Thomas Cahill, an expert on things Irish, who was quoted in the *New York Times* in June 1998, "You go to Italy, and they're just nuts for Irish music right now," so perhaps those Bologna informants of fall 1997 were optimistic about klezmer's efflorescence.

An appeal to the transnational can take many forms. On a broadcast celebration for Israel's fiftieth anniversary, sponsored by the United Jewish Appeal (April 16, 1998), the Hollywood Jewish organizers were eager to manufacture moments of overlap between America and Israel. They came up with elaborately produced birthday greetings from Texas cowboys, Maine barbers, and the president of the United States. Among the musical offerings, they arranged a side-by-side interaction between a bluegrass band and the Klezmer Conservatory Band (KCB). Unlike the far-fetched circuitry linking the Texas A & M line-dancing team and the State of Israel, the assumed parallelism between bluegrass and klezmer almost seemed natural. Yet it was a moment of cultural overload. Klezmer here stood in for Jewishness all right (we are back to the "national"), what bandleader Hankus Netsky, consultant to the show, called "a musical aspect of Jewish America," but how is this tied to celebrating Israel? Presumably through the choice of "Hava Nagila" as the highlighted tune. Somehow, in this context, bluegrass as all-American represented the mainstream and the subculture enjoying each other's difference. In fact, this is exactly how the bluegrass band saw it. In an e-mail message to a bluegrass website, Mike Bub of the Del McCoury Band describes being booked for the show, then says: "Our role will be to play against a Klezmer group from Boston. What this means is we will be representing American Music. . . . This could be big. Hell, it is BIG!!"

If an American show makes the equation bluegrass = American and klezmer = Israel, we have some very messy nesting and overlapping of categories. The klezmer musicians (a mix of Jews and non-Jews) feel they are American, and Israelis are not likely to see the KCB as a logo of their country. Yet the celebration was sponsored by media-conscious American Jews, who are apparently comfortable with this arrangement. Since their basic orientation was toward *Fiddler on the Roof,* according to Netsky (personal communication, 1999), even introducing klezmer shows how iconic it has become as a contemporary representation of identity.[1]

Before leaving the klezmer–bluegrass conjuncture, we should note an insider's voice to get a more immediate sense of how being pigeonholed affects musicians, as related by Judy Bressler, the vocalist of the KCB:

> We were "too Jewish" to play our own four-minute set. Even there, they were afraid people wouldn't be able to deal with it, and they'd switch the channel and watch *Chicago Hope.* It was a very, very frustrating experience for me personally. They chopped up what we did. They had the band play "Tzena, Tzena," [an early Israeli settler song popularized in America by the Weavers] no vocal, just the little instrumental piece of it, and out of nowhere, out of context, I'm singing a piece of "Romania, Romania" [a Yiddish vaudeville song], no context, no explanation. I think the bluegrass group got the better end of it in terms of coverage, in terms of time allotment, because they were more "normal." The first day, I called home, I was upset, crying upset, I said to my husband, "Eighteen years, and here's a major event, and we still can't really get the message out. We can't really show people what we do, or play people what we play, because we're too Jewish. That show no way promoted klezmer music, but I can't tell you how many people have come up and said, "I saw that." People are still coming up; it's been almost a month. (Interview with Mark Slobin, 1998)

To summarize this issue of klezmer as a transnational style, I've introduced polar examples. In the case of the Israeli celebration, klezmer and bluegrass are chips in a political and ideological game of public relations and prestige within a system of rational ordering of heritage musics. The Italian enthusiastic free-spirited response to klezmer seems in another cultural space altogether, having to do with expanding musical horizons, more involved with taste than politics. Still, both examples invoke a transnational circulation of musics that depends on mediated forms and an ideology of open borders and free exchange of cultural goods. It is in these senses and others listed above that understanding a system of overlaps seems a necessary step in giving klezmer a context.[2]

Some final points about overlaps might round out this study of klezmer's context. Beyond the heritage system, klezmer overlaps many other sectors of the music cultures in which it is embedded. Jazz remains one of the oldest and most durable of linkages, going back to the shifts from European to American instrumental and rhythmic stylings in early klezmer recordings. Eighty years after Lt. Joseph Frankel's recording of

"Yidishe Blues," a mother writing to me about her teenage son's musical interests says the boy is "hoping to pursue a career either in ethnomusicology or music history with an emphasis in Jewish music and jazz. . . . He follows jazz and klezmer avidly and is fascinated with the lore that surrounds them" (e-mail, 1998). The pairing is extremely tight here, with jazz and klezmer acting as parallel rails on which the boy's musical urge rides. This student has an unusually urgent sense of the importance of overlaps, as he is studying both German and Hebrew to get maximum leverage on Yiddish culture. Such planned dovetailing is an explicit version of the implicit strategies Jews have adopted for centuries.

THERE IS NO QUESTION that klezmer overlaps many of the basic parameters of the transatlantic heritage music system. The fit is tight for some, sloppy for others, and marginal for a few of the complementary factors. Inside the peripheral tangents and spheres, a klezmer core remains untouched by comparativism. The overlaps provide bridges to the core that both outsiders and insiders traverse in search of nostalgia or novelty, tradition or trade.

The core sustains its distinctiveness because the Jews do. Non-Jews have a multiple, fragmented consciousness about the Jews, as any example of musical contact like the bluegrass–klezmer moment, or a Berlin audience going to a klezmer event, will show. There are no other heritage musics that can draw an audience from motives ranging from sheer show biz through expiation of your grandfathers' sins, and the same is true for reasons to play the music.

This distinction would be reason enough for klezmer to be a special case, but there is also the other side of the cultural dialogue to take into account: the Jews themselves are just as multilateral in thinking about and playing this heritage music. Any given band, as we will see in the next chapter, might function in extremely varied ways yet keep its identity under the klezmer umbrella. Collectively, klezmer fills not just one recognizable cultural niche, but a whole set of complementary or even competing subniches that together form a core that looks like a fly's eye: an incredibly multifaceted surface that both takes in and reflects meaning from its environment, adjusting to changing events even while staying focused on its main objective—sustenance and survival.

The following chapters will view klezmer at work, first reflecting more fully on why people move toward it, then surveying its settings, and finally turning to the sonic materials that provide the musical and cultural resonance of klezmer.

3

Klezmer as an Urge

This chapter grapples with some of the driving forces behind klezmer affiliation, especially for the musicians who invest their creativity, energy, and time into this subcommodified, tenuous line of work. I looked for background factors that occur in all klezmer contexts, trying to find footholds in the face of a whirlwind of musical activity. The ingredients listed here do not form a standard recipe, since the percentage each takes up in the finished product—concert, album, career, fan allegiance—varies wildly from case to case. I will look at four factors: marketing, musical magnetism, personal pathways, and the power of evocation.

Marketing

Things have changed in the marketing of klezmer. In the 1920s and 1930s the great clarinetist Dave Tarras hid behind various names to pose as a Greek or Polish musician for recording purposes, part of a general pattern of Jews doing studio work for other ethnic groups' listening pleasure. There were also humdrum contractual issues that caused name changes. Hankus Netsky, whose pioneering klezmer research is cited throughout this book, reports the following exchange with Mel Davis, "a Philadelphia trumpeter who went on to a big career in New York":

> I wanted to know more about the personnel on a Harry Ringler klezmer collection which I suspected he was on, as Moshe Davis. I guessed everyone had other contracts, so they all changed their names. "So who was Danny Albert?" "That would be Dave Tarras." "And the drummer, Sticks Cohen?" "That would be Bobby Rosengarden." "And the accordionist, Izzie Koretsky?" "That would be Dominic Cortese."

I forgot to ask about the arranger, Yossel Cain, but I can assume it was Henry Mancini. (Netsky, personal communication)

It is hard to imagine anyone in today's klezmer world changing his or her name for any reason, contractual, ethnic, or personal. The marketing of klezmer has grown increasingly sophisticated as the young generation of revivalists slowly goes gray. German managers offer American bands real-world advice about ownership of songs and arrangements. This move toward outside expertise was unknown in the early fraternal days of the budding klezmer movement. The search and struggle for better-paying gigs and choicer venues become more serious as the market broadens for the music. Issues of artistic direction become more entangled with finding an audience. This does not mean a crass scramble for markets has broken out; on the contrary, musicians may try to set their own terms ever more carefully.

Since the marketing of heritage musics has hardly been studied, a comparative move won't help here, except intuitively. At the level of meeting audience expectation, klezmer is clearly just one of a vast set of musics extending across Eurasia that features a small band hired for specific celebrations who will be valued primarily for two things: a large repertoire and a steady beat. I found the same pattern in fieldwork in Afghanistan (1967–1972) in that others have reported for the Balkans and Appalachia. Today's klezmer bands must meet those same requirements and often depend on exactly the same kinds of events—weddings in particular—as did their artistic ancestors. Descriptions of how people got started as performers usually include a musician's discovery that one could get paid to play this music. Here's a typical quote from an interview with a prominent American musician: "There was a sign in the music department there asking if someone wanted to play Jewish music, and I went, and I met A.B., who had long been involved in Balkan music, and I started playing with [his band], and we did weddings and concerts."

Once hooked on the klezmer life, musicians discover the perils and pleasures of subcommodification. Like local American polka bands or other heritage groups, local or low-level klezmer ensembles generate albums more for publicity than for sales. Few klezmer releases sell more than a couple of thousand copies, not enough to live on royalties. Less prominent bands might reach the 10,000–15,000-copy level, so it is only a small group of elite bands that can expect minimum sales of 40,000–50,000 copies and the expectation that their albums will stay in the bins for several years. It will remain hard to match Itzhak Perlman's 200,000-plus sale figure for his first klezmer CD. The star bands that traveled with Perlman found their pay envelopes much fatter than when they toured on their own. In the klezmer world we do not find the type of extraordinary energy toward breaking into the dominant record industry that marks the strivings of other heritage-based musics, such as the Asian Americans Deborah Wong describes. She says they are not "interested in creating something that is aurally recognizable as an Asian American sound; rather, almost all such cultural workers are interested in the political and artistic potential of Asian Americans who could change social land- and soundscapes with their mere presence" (Wong 1997:294). This is a statement of "minority" thinking that is unlikely to emerge from Jewish Americans, who have been given special deracialized status as "whites" and who achieved prominence within the dominant recording industry generations back.

For klezmer, far more common than plans for media marketing is the strategizing of the local working band, which features the eclectic mix of musics that klezmorim have always offered the paying public. It is hard to tell "klezmer" bands from general "Jewish" bands, which have always existed locally and who are now using the word "klezmer" as part of marketing. Here is a random example, from the San Francisco Bay area (*Jewish Bulletin of Northern California*, April 24, 1998):

"The Shtetlblasters: From Jerusalem to Motown"

"Hot Borscht: Music with a Beet—Israeli Folk, Klezmer, Ballroom, Pop & Top 40"

"California Klezmer: Klezmer & Yiddish Music for All Occasions—Traditional dance music & songs, 50's & 60's, Rock n' Roll, Swing. Acoustic music—our specialty"

"Adama: Music of the Jewish People"

"Gordon Fels and music associates: Premium Entertainment with a Jewish Touch"

"Joel Abramson Orchestras: Solos to Bands, D-J Band Combinations—Bar/Bat Mitzvahs; Weddings; Corporate"

While not all of these use the term "klezmer," something klezmer-like will almost certainly appear on the playlists of all these ensembles, given the music's infiltration into everyday Jewish-American life. Klezmer's other side, as an American countercultural music, might push musicians to buck the marketing trend, to define themselves as artists who play only a given core klezmer repertoire. An interesting moment arose at the 1996 Wesleyan Klezmer Research Conference when Kurt Bjorling spoke about his aesthetic stand. Bjorling, a member of Brave Old World and founder of his own Chicago Klezmer Ensemble, is an outspoken purist. He went so far as to say: "I'm not a klezmer. If I were, I'd be playing the 'Macarena' [a hot dance craze] at weddings." True enough—to be a klezmer traditionally meant, and still tends to mean, playing whatever the paying customers want to listen and dance to. The Macarena is just a more modern version of whatever trendy toe-tapping number the wedding guests would request in 1820 or 1920.

Aggressive bands can discover that there are niches everywhere in the American live music market, spaces just big enough for them to fit into, as reported by Glenn Hartman of the New Orleans Klezmer All-Stars:

> Because we tour like an indie rock band, and we're always looking for a venue to get into, sometimes the most logical place will be the alternative venue in town where they get a lot of ska acts, or punk acts, so we get to be the category where the people that normally listen to ska can find some sort of common ground with our fast two beat. "Wow, this stuff is frenetic and fast, high energy," so they get grabbed by it when they wouldn't normally listen to a Yiddish band, especially if you were going to present us in a synagogue or a JCC.
>
> So we'll have these days where we have a combination of gigs. Oh we're going to play, first we'll play at a university for some class, then we'll play at the Louisiana State Museum for a bunch of kids, and we'll get 200 African-American fifth graders in a situation where their principal is saying, "I can't believe you did this; I can't believe the kids are moved by this music," and then we'll go to an alternative rock club and it'll be two in the morning and the women will be taking off their clothes and belly dancing, and it'll be the same music. [MS: Do you adjust the music to the site?] Not really. Maybe the dynamic level; it's louder in some places, maybe we choose the song a little bit differently, but primarily we play the same stuff. (Interview, 1998)

Marketing configures closely with regional life, part of the community setting we'll look at more closely in the next chapter. In their promotional newsletter of November 1998, The Kabalas, an Iowa band, trumpet that they are "together at last" with Rudy Hodnik, "the area's premiere accordion polka king!" This kind of coziness extends to their planning of the fourth annual pajama party, held at the local library, where the sales pitch includes "Kabalas Glow-In-The-Dark Nightshirts." Slowly klezmer marketing is moving not just geographically, but generationally, as the emergence of "Oy Vey! Young People's Klezmer Workshop" shows. Billed as "a totally cool klezmer experience for kids," the CD version of the show boasts blurbs like this one: "I want to grab every Jewish parent and grandparent and tell them to run out and buy this album for their children and grandchildren," from Rabbi Vivian Mayer of Danbury, Connecticut.

How much marketing determines musical and career choices remains open to question and is the sort of interview question ethnographers hate to ask and musicians don't like to answer or have quoted. In this, klezmer is no different from other heritage, or even popular, musics. Certainly bands position themselves. The young Italian musicians I interviewed in Bologna (1997) belong to several overlapping bands, some playing klezmer and others a variety of heritage musics, and the same was true for a Berlin group I talked to. Klezmer can be just one option in the overlap system, which might include not just heritage styles, but also jazz or classical as other possibilities for getting paid jobs. Sometimes crossing genre boundaries can put a musician on someone else's turf. Nico Staiti, an Italian ethnomusicologist who works with Roma ("gypsy") musicians, said he was with a group of his informants in Milan when they chanced upon a klezmer band playing in the street. The Roma were outraged—"But they're playing our music!"

The wider the recognition, the higher the stakes become in the search for market positioning. In 1997 the Krakow band Kroke were quite excited about signing with Peter Gabriel's WOMAD organization, which gave them access to world music festival audiences and the Real World record label, widely distributed in major record store chains. They did not talk about how their music-making itself connected with this breakthrough, though it was clear to me that they were trying hard to develop a sound that would be perhaps ethnic but would not remind listeners too much of the major American klezmer bands. The band members had grown up together, playing classical, jazz, and folk music as youngsters, and had only recently moved into klezmer. In the process of klezmerizing, two of the band members reported, they discovered that they actually come from Jewish families, a remarkable coincidence that offered some authenticity to the mix as well as providing a different point of connection to the klezmer world: memory, which will be discussed later.

The point about marketing as a motivation is not to approach it cynically, as either insider or outside observer. It is rarely the sole driving force. If it does provide the initial impetus for musicians' moves, they find more compelling reasons to stick with it and hone their skills. These reasons can be musical but are often emotional as well.

Musical Magnetism

The opposite of marketing might be a completely unprovoked affinity for the music itself, so often cited by people telling how they got into klezmer. Their stories about hearing as revelation, as opening the ears to a hidden but now urgent message, link klezmer closely to the experiences of the Balkan enthusiasts mentioned earlier who described being struck by musical lightning. But without the next step, finding out there's a way to play this music profitably, most musicians would never have followed this piper down the pathway of career commitment. For listeners, the moment of recognition and attachment can surely be both accidental and meaningful, but the album or concert that provokes the discovery has the hook for their receptor.

Klezmer has strong powers of attraction. In the absence of convincing historical contact, it would otherwise be hard to explain why Finns, Italians, and Australians immediately feel its pull. Even for Americans, klezmer has little or no obvious claim on their attention, since it is just one item in their shopping cart of musics. So varieties of attraction and concentration become important for analyzing this microsystem. The field of this magnetic pull is very wide. At one end, perhaps, lies the thunderclap experience, the moment of revelation that "this is the music I've been waiting for." For musicians, there are many slower and more subtle lines of force that draw them toward the core of this music. Much of this attraction has to do with how klezmer fits into their well-established musical models and skills. Klezmer can be an extension of or a great relief from what a musician is used to playing, or both of these at the same time. In interviews in America and Europe, among both experienced and new klezmer musicians, I hear about the mental and musical reshaping the music causes for those grounded in classical, ethnic, or jazz styles. A quote from a classically trained American violinist will give some idea of the process:

> If I'm playing a Bach sonata, I'm like, I have diarrhea, I'm nervous the whole day, I have to take three baths, and then I do it, and then I go, I guess that was fun . . . but when I play this stuff, I get excited, I'm a little nervous, but it's nothing like when I play some of what we call the old masters. (Marlene "Cookie" Segelstein, interview, 1997)

We don't have much literature on personal perestroika, the reconfiguring of muscles and meanings musicians experience when they add new styles. Encountering something new forces a reevaluation of the older layers, putting everything into question. Here musical magnetism is a catalyst for change. This need for musical metamorphosis must be one of the main reasons for the spread of a style-complex like klezmer. After becoming "addicted," as one violinist put it, musicians appreciate the fact that reshaping their musical world was itself a necessity. To cite another violinist, consider again Itzhak Perlman, who moved from a modest interest in klezmer to a deep appreciation of the music's technical demands and expressive power. In the film *In the Fiddler's House* (1995), about Perlman's move into the klezmer world, several scenes reveal the celebrity violinist being surprisingly candid about showing his surprise and even discomfiture when faced with the skills of top klezmer stars. Purely at the level of professionalism, he found himself practicing to perfect an appropriate response and an adequate personal style for this magnetic music he had encountered almost casually.

Once a mantle of prestige begins to descend on a music for whatever reasons, its magnetism grows. By 1998 the first prize in the International New Music Competition of the American Society for Jewish Music could be awarded to Harold Seletsky for his *Concertino for Klezmer Clarinet and String Quartet*. The award citation says: "Seletsky, a virtuoso clarinetist as well as composer, has written an extraordinary score that pulls out all the stops for the Klezmer player and . . . is an exciting addition to the growing number of works of this nature by composers." This statement from a panel of "distinguished musicologists and composers" measures the magnitude of the attractive power of a music once considered beneath the serious clarinetist's contempt. Klezmer star David Krakauer also operates at the highest level of classical clarinetism, and told me that jazz great Sidney Bechet informs all his work. A comment like this helps measure the distance covered since the late 1970s, when klezmer clarinet master Dave Tarras had to be coaxed by revivalists into bringing his klezmer skills back to consciousness.

Prestige levels of magnetism are still rare. Much more commonly, the attraction to klezmer represents an overlap from other force fields within the "traditional" set of musics. The band from Bologna all came from adjacent systems and intuited klezmer as a logical extension of styles they and their audience are used to. They noticed that when they play in southern Italy, even black-clad old women get up to dance, and the dance they do is the tarantella. Perceptively, the Bolognese have observed that the basically duple-meter core of klezmer dance tunes move people to get up on their feet in the south, whereas listeners in northern Italy, more accustomed to triple-meter dances like the waltz, are less likely to dance in the aisles. The Bolognese also pointed to the Balkan relationship; for Italy, Balkan music is not as exotic as it is for Americans or Swedes. In Berlin, where Balkan music was fairly rare until recently, a young klezmer musician told me that she moved from klezmer to Balkan, which she didn't know before, because of the similarities. Once in a magnetic field, you become aware of others pulling you in nearby directions.

Maybe it's just that people have musical "types," the way they do in choosing love partners. Just as you might scan the sea of faces for attractive features, gaits, and ways of speaking, the appearance of musics on the scene may provoke similar affinity moves. Once drawn in, you find out that magnetism and marketing tend to walk just a few steps apart. But there is much more to this choice than a simple setup of acquaintance, recognition, and negotiation, and it is to these more problematic areas that we turn next in looking for major motivating forces behind the klezmer system.

Personal Pathways

I've just suggested how some of these work: the specific pull of musics, the ways that klezmer can act as an extension of what you know, or the recognition that you can find an audience for the skills you've developed. In these ways, klezmer is little different from many heritage musics or other micromusical forms around today. But interviews bring out the very individual, deeply personal ways that klezmer is intertwined with biographies. Layer upon layer of sensibility, experience, and emotion combine to form a klezmer musician or klezmerophile listener. Since it is impossible credibly to characterize whole strata of performers and their audiences, a useful strategy might be to present chapters of the narrative of a selected subset, four American women violinists in their early thirties at interview time. This is hardly a statistical sample, but the issues raised by their remarks might resonate with the larger vibrations of the klezmer community of a certain generation and orientation.

■　　■　　■

Marlene "Cookie" Segelstein, born in 1958, currently playing with a Connecticut klezmer band, The Klezical Tradition, as well as in classical music ensembles:

I'm really Golda-Malke [her Hebrew name], but I didn't realize that until I had children. I'm a first-generation American, so in a lot of ways I've been a parent to my parents. They were learning English as I was learning English; they were speaking Hungarian and Yiddish when I was growing up in Kansas City; they came over in 1948. There's a certain attitude among European Jews that American Jews are goyim. We never had American Jewish friends . . . it was amazing to me when I was five or six that there were Jewish Americans; I expected to see a cross in their home . . . my mother said, "Well, one step above the goyim."

I remember my father humming these tunes, like "Sha Shtil" [a well-known Yiddish song], . . . but I have to drag it out of him; he doesn't want to go back to that world (Czechoslovakia, Carpathian Ruthenia, now it's Ukraine; my mother was from Munkacs). . . . My father, even when I was doing this music, said, "You don't have to do this music, why are you doing this music; that's what we did because we couldn't do anything else."

I grew up with this very rich traditional stuff, but with these people really trying to assimilate into Kansas City. . . . There was my house, this little Europe, and there was the Midwest . . . I had safety in one world from the other. . . . I was one of two Jews in my class . . . at times I didn't even want to deal with being Jewish there; I wanted to be just another cowgirl.

Embedded in the European Jewish orientation of Cookie's parents was the belief in classical music as a desirable skill:

> I was always a real classical musician, had violin lessons forced down my throat, switched to viola in high school, loved the viola. . . . I ask my father, what did the [klezmer] violinists sound like, and he says, "Ekh!" and that the violinist never took a bath . . . they were just the necessary evils that had to be there; he says his grandmother was afraid of them; never let them into the house because they might take something.

Overcoming her father's disgust, Cookie found herself drawn into klezmer as a new avenue for her violin:

> I had played a little klezmer earlier, maybe '89; I didn't perceive it as a different way of playing my violin. It was a slow process, but it was as if I kind of got sucked from one world and put myself in another world. The music is a natural medium for my growth. It's been a safe medium, because I don't have to talk. . . . I think that the people who understand the vulnerability I'm showing, I'm a little safer than if I just spewed it verbally.

From the violinistic to the personal is not much of a leap, since the instrument is already deeply internalized; it is the tunes themselves that make the bridge stable:

> I'm always saying, how old is this tune, and what that's saying for me is, how far back does this go in my roots, how far back can I say this is part of me, this is who I am, this is who my people are, and this gives me emotional stability. Some people can say, my ancestors came over on the Mayflower, and I can say—this tune is 150 years old. . . . that's my Mayflower, I guess.
>
> My priorities have completely turned around. I made my first Passover dinner in '92, began asking why am I doing this? Why do I want to be Jewish? I started looking for a synagogue. It was like I had a twin that was doing this for me. But now I'm intrigued with that, it's like a juicy gravy, I crave that stuff. My husband says he doesn't know me, he says what happened to the atheist I married?

Despite the seeming stability the music offers her, Cookie is still drawn to the edginess that infused her parents' house, which she says is essential to *yiddishkayt,* the Jewishness of the tunes and their affective charge:

I think [the music] has a certain desperation, a desperate quality, like a Czech movie. . . . There's a real taste of I guess sadness would be the right word, loss . . . even in the happiest of it there's a twinkling in the recognition of suffering; we can enjoy this for now, but we have to keep an eye on the door. . . . I was definitely brought up that way . . . you can enjoy the flowers, but you better come back in soon. I remember Raphael Hilyer [viola teacher] said—I was playing one of the Bach suites, a sarabande—. . . he said, "You know, this doesn't have to suffer." . . . It was kind of a minor key; I didn't even know it. He said it can be in a minor key and it doesn't have to be like death is approaching.

Gender is another variable in the personal equation:

[MS: Why are there women becoming prominent playing the fiddle in klezmer?] There's a certain vulnerability about this music, and maybe that has something to do with it. I mean, women will certainly show their vulnerability to their friends more than men will. . . . This is not really athletic music [like classical]; it's more of an exploration of the female side of everybody.

■   ■   ■

Deborah Strauss, born in 1966, a very visible veteran klezmer violinist:

I started violin at 6 in Buffalo because my father played the violin and he had a violin his father brought from Poland. My father spoke Yiddish when he was a little boy, but we didn't by any means have a Yiddish-associated household. [Her family kept kosher, she went to Hebrew day school, everything was focused on Israel and Zionism.] So all the stuff I've brought back now to my parents, it's new to them, in a sense.

[After some early exposure to klezmer playing in an amateur band] I met Michael Alpert, this is 1985, I was 19 years old. I played for him, and even then he said, "Your technique is so much better than mine, I don't know what I can tell you." I didn't get connected with the people who could open up resources for me. I happened to find my way to the University of Chicago and went to graduate school there. I had no concept of wanting to find out about ethnomusicology. [She studied with Kurt Bjorling there, deepening her knowledge about klezmer style] so I knew physically a little what to do. . . . I took a leave of absence from school in the fall and I went to Klezkamp for the first time—that was in '92 , really not that long ago.

Unlike Cookie Segelstein, Deborah Strauss tapped into klezmer through well-grounded mentors, Alpert and Bjorling, and noticed the importance of immersion at Klezkamp, the central switching-station. Still, she does not simply follow her teachers but rather her intuition and her violinism as she moves inquiringly along her personal pathway:

Klezmer brought me a whole new way of thinking about my instruments. I started from scratch; I would practice what I needed to practice in order to be able to execute. . . . It was a revelation to me, a whole new way to practice. . . . I wasn't even transcribing the tunes. . . . It transformed the way I think about music. It was a fresh relationship; it wasn't burdened with years of expectation and disappointment and pressure; it was what it was, and it was so beautiful; it was this uncharted world . . . it saved my playing . . . it just opened up my ears and my mind . . . and then it becomes an addiction. [After intensive listening to the 78 RPM recordings] you go back to it a year later, and it sounds completely different. You hear 20 percent more of what they're doing.

There's the way I can talk about this that's emotional, what was my connection, and how I got inside these tunes, and I played it, and people responded to it, they said, "This sounds good, this sounds right. . . ." Then there's this level of like what does this mean, and how do I explain it, what's right and what's wrong, and what am I teaching, the theory and the way you describe it, the way you position yourself, and it's a real battle for me, actually.

■ ■ ■

Alicia Svigals, born in 1963, founding member of the Klezmatics, a top klezmer band internationally:

In 1986 when I graduated college I answered an ad in the village voice that a clarinetist named Rob Chavez who had been in a klezmer band in California had placed to form a klezmer band. He disappeared after a few months but that's what got the Klezmatics together. But before that I went to the Workmen's Circle school [an old-time Jewish socialist organization that stressed Yiddish language and a secular approach to Jewish identity] when I was a kid, where I acquired a reading knowledge of Yiddish and we learned a bunch of Yiddish folk songs, or what are thought of as folk songs.

I grew up with some WEVD, "the station that speaks your language." So my father always put on the radio. They played a lot of folk songs, cantorial music, Jan Bart [a Yiddish crooner], everything but klezmer music because at that time it wasn't happening.

My father was the supervisor of arts programing for the school district in Spanish Harlem, so there was some money for these things, so he employed among other people Andy Statman's wife, Barbara, and Andy [a major figure on the klezmer scene since mid-1970s] used to come over to our house and he turned me on to klezmer at the time when he was just getting into it and I was a teenager, so there was a family connection. So when I saw this ad, I said "My God, this is the stuff Andy does, how incredible," so that's how I started. I did the YIVO summer program and I met Henry [Sapoznik, important New York klezmer figure and founder of Klezkamp], and Henry told me about Klezkamp, so I went to Klezkamp the following year and then I began teaching at Klezkamp.

I started [on the violin] when I was 5. My great-grandparents were from Odessa. There was like a fiddle thing in the air, they told me. Basically they put a little fiddle in my hands and said, "You will now take fiddle lessons like everybody else." I practiced, and I hated it. This was in 1968. Then when I was a teenager I went to music camp. That was a brilliant move on my parents' part. I was into heavy metal and trying to smoke pot, so I came back, cut my hair, cleaned up my act. I was into the chamber music scene. So I gave my heavy metal albums to my brother. But they came back when the Klezmatics started; all that heavy metal came back.

Family influences and connections set up a tug-of-war with the pull of pop music, but this dialectic is only part of Svigals's musical odyssey, which detours through music camp to the countercultural scene on the streets of New York and Europe:

Actually what really happened was when I was 16 we moved to the city (I grew up in Spring Valley) and I started to play on the streets to earn money to go to music camp, this fabulous music camp, and I met these Italian bluegrass musicians; they were part of this Italian bluegrass craze that was going on in Italy, old-timey, and they hardly spoke English; they would sing "Rrroll on buddy, rroll on." So like we traded English lessons for bluegrass lessons. So they got me into this folk music thing. The banjo player in particular had this Marxist interpretation of music, and as an impressionable 16-year old I was right there. I was like, "I love Brahms, I love Beethoven," and he said "But Alicia, that is the music of the bourgeoisie. That is the music of the oppressor class, and bluegrass is the music of the people." And I was like, God, he's right, look at Lincoln Center. So I totally got out of classical music—I was a confused teenager—and totally got into folk music.

I dropped out of college for a while and went hitchhiking around Europe. I went with $10, literally, with my fiddle, because I had been playing in the streets of New York and was into being this hippie musician. I traveled for a year hitchhiking and playing in the streets and supporting myself that way. I met a lot of people from different places playing different kinds of music and we all played together. I made tapes of this—terrible tapes. So I played with Berber musicians in France, this Minorcan folksinger in Barcelona, it was really fun. It was 1983 and there was a folk revival happening all over the world. This wasn't like a little Minorcan lady; it was somebody starting the Minorcan folk music revival. And the same with the Berbers. I ran into all these Italians who were following the folk music revival group. So when I came home, like Henry [Sapoznik] and everybody else, I decided to get into my own folk music. When I read that ad, it really appealed to me. But by that time I already had my self-definition as a musician, a folk music hippie, before the world music turn. I was interested in world music before anyone else I knew was.

Svigals finally grounded her huge set of musical experiences and resources in the identification with Yiddish culture she got early in childhood. Like her other colleagues in the Klezmatics, she envisions her evolution as a process of flowing forward personally and artistically as part of a confluence of herself and the tradition.

This thing steamrollered. It's always been something I wanted to do. I'm Jewish and I identify with Yiddish, not Hebrew, with the old socialism of my grandparents. Klezmer is the musical department of that because it's the music of the people, it harkens back to that stuff, the Yiddish stuff. It's available to be projected onto.

From our point of view as musicians, as artists, as someone who wants to have an integrated view of what we do, and like a rationale for it, what we say is we want to be authentic. Not in a musically false sense of fetishized slice of musical life from recordings, but in the psychoanalytic sense of being true to yourself. So we want to have an authentic way to be musically Jewish. We're going to draw on whatever materials are available and appeal to us. And then we're going to make something new out of them.

We want to have our own musical language for instrumentalists. We come from jazz background, I was into Irish for a while, bluegrass, and here's something that's analogous to that. This is my own instrumental musical language, complex, rich, deep, interesting, emotional—

great! that's available. So as a Jew, as an Ashkenazic Jew even, I take klezmer music.

Basically I'm self-taught. I basically culled what I thought the style was from old fiddle recordings, all the living and dead musicians I came in contact with, and I feel I've really created my own klezmer fiddle style. I think it can be called a method for klezmer; hopefully that's what every musician does.

As much as Svigals's trajectory seems to suit a child of the sixties and seventies, in some basic ways it is reminiscent of the kinds of things older musicians say about their musical pathways. An example is the venerable Max Epstein, born in 1912: "I played with the best of them. I got a little of this guy, a little of this guy, I put them together, and I try to make the best out of all of them" (1999 interview with Hankus Netsky). Of course, Epstein played live with the klezmer greats, but his attitude of constructive eclecticism and stylistic individuality built on "all the living and dead musicians I came in contact with," to use Svigals's phrase, remains the central sensibility of today's leading musicians.

■   ■   ■

Laurie Tanenbaum, born in 1961, founder of the Santa Cruz, California, band Hoo-tza-tza:

When I was in first grade in Puerto Rico, my mom taught me folk guitar, folk songs, and Beatles songs, and then in second grade we went back to Cleveland. Second grade I started music theory . . . in third grade I started violin lessons through the Cleveland Institute of Music. Straight classical, and I was still playing folk guitar, and then with violin it was classical, and I played in the school orchestra. I was interested in folk music and other musics, but I didn't exactly know how that connected to the violin. . . . I bought a book I actually use now with students on Appalachian folk fiddling. I sort of worked on that book on my own, but my teachers didn't even know I was doing that, so I kept doing violin lessons.

I had exposure to Jewish music through my parents. They had Theodore Bikel records, so I grew up with some of that stuff, hearing it on guitar. They had quite a few of them, so I really got to hear a lot of them, but I didn't connect that with the violin.

[After college, having moved to Santa Cruz] I wanted to learn more about improvisation, so I thought, well, the area in the United States that's most about improvisation is jazz, so I got seriously into jazz with Ray Brown, who's a jazz educator at Cabrillo College. I just started living and breathing jazz. Once I started doing that, I started to fall in love with jazz, so I started this jazz immersion thing. I must have done the jazz combos at least eight times, writing for jazz combo, writing for big band, so I wrote for big band, you're writing for a twenty-piece band. Also chamber music, and playing in pit orchestra for shows around here, still playing with people at parties.

By now the familiar multimusicality so much a part of the American experience should strike the reader. Now we expect a turning point to occur:

Then it reached a point where I was doing all those things, then I decided to go to graduate school in music at San Jose State, because it was nearby. I got into the master's program there. I had to study a lot on my own about music history to take all those exams. I was studying more on classical violin to learn more about my technique. I was playing in the Santa Cruz Symphony, and I was playing chamber music and jazz jobs. I had to take the core curriculum, and I was learning all about this church, and that pope, and I thought—I want to learn more about klezmer music. I was having to spend so much time on this stuff that wasn't even the kind of music [I wanted to play].

As in the previous interviews, the turn toward klezmer led to a search for authoritative sources. In this case the young violinist found Svigals, who has now become a major mentor herself. Kurt Bjorling and Klezkamp make a return appearance as well:

I approached it first very academically—what can I find out about this? In this research I found out about YIVO, so I decided I had to go to New York to do my research. I actually flew to New York so I could go to the YIVO library there. I go to YIVO and I go to the library, and then I'm in the lobby area, and there's this woman who's very friendly, and I'm chatting with her, and she turns out to be Alicia Svigals, who's around my age. It was the best thing that happened to me. [Svigals put her in touch with Kurt Bjorling; Tanenbaum went to Klezkamp and studied with Svigals.]

SURVEYING THESE INTERVIEW EXCERPTS, it should be clear that each woman has arrived at the klezmer violin from different personal and musical pathways and has a distinctive attitude shaped by those experiences and her own temperament. The networks of the klezmer world shine through the surface variation, particularly the mentoring linkages.

One factor in particular dominates all these narratives: the cultural freedom Jewish Americans have to experiment with their feelings of belonging, part of the musical license American society offers to make full use of one's talents. Being self-taught figures in the life of countless American subcultural and countercultural musicians, sometimes worn as a badge of pride. In Europe the well-entrenched systems of music schooling have often meant that musicians, including some of today's klezmorim, might well come from a conservatory background. Also apparent is the compressed time frame of the accounts—the klezmer activity is all within the last decade, at the very most—putting this micromusic squarely within more universal trends. All music systems these days, including those most commodified (rap, dance music), move at an almost dizzying speed through quick-switching generations of leadership and aesthetics. Music systems have always been in a constant state of evolution, but the acceleration in turnover of taste now seems to be routine.

The Power of Evocation

In many—but certainly not all—cases, response to klezmer has something to do with its evocative power. What is being evoked is not unambiguous nor does it lack irony. Perhaps the concept can best be understood through its opposite: the power of nonevocation, so common in certain types of popular music and nicely summarized in the 1998 obituary of Bob Merrill, who wrote such nonevocative hits as "If I Knew You Were Coming I'd've Baked a Cake." He is quoted as saying this about his hits: "They are all about America, they are all wholesome, and they are all happy." While this attitude does betray an interest in the evocation of an ideology, the songs' power deliberately emanates from the most neutral cultural materials. The *New York Times* points out that "They made liberal use of cliches, as Mr. Merrill cheerfully admitted, telling how he filled notebooks with them. 'Cliches make the best songs,' he said, 'I put down every one I can find.'"

Set against this all-American blackboard, the white chalk of heritage affirmation stands out vividly, but it is not easy to decipher the cultural hieroglyph of klezmer. In a facile way, it can be read off the surface of newspaper reviews, liner notes, poster copy, and other such public pronouncements and interpreted at face value. More buried, tributes to the power of evocation lurk in the narratives people offer about what draws them to this heritage music. In a short account, I will offer some intuitions based on decades of observing why people like certain musics and on the ways Jewish-oriented expressive forms play themselves out in public.

A sense of Jewishness and its historical fate is not hard to locate, sometimes near the heart of klezmer. Here's what the young musicians of Bologna's band Dire-gelt had to say about their foray into klezmer, which they describe as a step-by-step process by complete outsiders feeling their way into a foreign music-cultural space:

> At the beginning, actually, we were attracted just by the music. But then, during our performances, there was always someone who asked, "are you Jewish?" So we started to ask the same question to ourselves.
>
> After the first moment, when we started to play, we realized there was something more behind the music. It wasn't just a kind of different culture than others; it was something quite more different. Up to now, we don't know what that is; there is a thing that is deeper. Everyone has a different reason and has followed a different path to Jewish culture. We know that Jewish culture means so many different things. (Interview, 1997)

It is no accident that several European bands, including this Bologna group on certain nights, use the name Goyim (non-Jews) as a way of situating themselves, even on albums and tours. Perhaps even mock-Jewishness invokes a certain irony appropriated from the group one is paying homage to.

This one example should be enough to give the reader an idea of the tangled paths musicians set out on when they devote themselves to klezmer. Why did the Italian audiences ask Dire-gelt, "Are you Jewish?" No one asks performers of Bach if they're German, or even whether members of American Sacred Harp hymn-singing groups are Protestants. Some heritage traditions are considered public property, while others are surrounded by a screen or a haze of authenticity that attracts the attention of even the least knowledgeable consumers. The term "evocation" is used here to try to neutralize this affect, but inevitably one has to confront the more charged term "memory." There's a large and rapidly growing literature around this term partly arising from the need for reevaluation that is at the heart of heritage moves, and it's happening in all corners of the cultural theory world. Postcolonial theory is loaded with notions of memory, with increasing attention paid to anniversaries, such as the fiftieth year of India's independence. In many European countries, marking fifty years from 1945, the end of World War II, became the occasion for much reflection about the road recently traveled. In the American Southwest, 1998 saw greater attention paid to the effects of the Gold Rush and the conquest of the region by the United States 150 years earlier, and so on. Public apologies for past collective wrongs have been coming forth regularly, ranging from the pope's regretting the anti-Semitism of the Catholic Church to the U.S. president's admitting American complicity in the African slave trade. Australia now has an official "Sorry Day" when the whole country is asked to reflect on the damage done to aboriginal peoples.

This sort of manifestation, and many more involving plaques, museums, stamp issues, and recording reissues, extends through the enormous increase in memoirs written not just by public figures and celebrities but also by scholars flaunting their subjectivity. The whole range of these phenomena has been dubbed *lieux de memoire* in the much-cited work of the French historian Pierre Nora (1994). Nora's thesis is that we no longer live in *milieux de memoire*, memory environments where memory is embedded into everyday life, so we create *lieux*, "places" of memory instead. There are certainly limits to adapting Nora's large-scale theoretical scaffolding for seven volumes commenting on French culture, since the work tends to refer to national rather than small-group ideas of memory. One can object that there are more "real" communities around than Nora implies, and can note that he is not interested in the kind of cross-community evocation klezmer produces. But his insights certainly carry a real interpretive charge for understanding heritage group behavior.

History and Memory in African-American Culture (Fabre and O'Meally 1994) tries to apply Nora's work to black contexts of memory. Three passages from the introduction suggest how close Nora's concerns, as extended by scholars working on an adjacent subculture, are to the production and reproduction of klezmer:

> We noted that certain sites of memory were sometimes constructed by one generation in one way and then reinterpreted by another. These sites may fall unexpectedly out of grace or be revisited suddenly, and brought back to life. We found the *lieux de memoire* are constantly evolving new configurations of meaning, and that their constant revision makes them part of the dynamism of the historical process. (Fabre and O'Meally 1994:8–9)

This could be a passage from an article on the evolution of klezmer as part of Jewish memory; indeed, it echoes most of the writing on klezmer, going back to 1984, when the movement first made its mark on public consciousness (Slobin 1984).

> Nor have we taken the easy way of approaching African Americans as a monolith. Our studies paid close attention to divisions within this deeply varied group. Sometimes, we noted, interactions within the veil of African America have concerned constituencies that are intimately related; then again, they have involved groups that hardly acknowledge each other. (Fabre and O'Meally 1994:8–9)

This recognition of internal difference is also critical to positioning klezmer within the Jewish world. Jewish subgroups don't just stay indifferent to each other but tend increasingly to become actively antagonistic. To the outsider, music might look like a common resource for various factions. One can hear some of the same tunes and see some of the same dance steps at Hasidic and secular Jewish weddings, and some musicians play both jobs. But few know about or emphasize this dovetailing. People, including musicians, invoke memory when they invent personal and group genealogies, which expands in-group diversity over time. Many shifting currents and sandbars wreck our interpretive moves. One more quotation from Fabre and O'Meally is strikingly parallel to klezmer: "It is clear enough that audiences varying in ethnic affiliation, class, gender, and/or location in space or time . . . will receive sometimes widely different messages from the coded texts we were studying" (ibid.). It is fascinating how closely this passage about the reception of African-American culture mirrors klezmer's mobility. The "coded texts" musicians produce move freely across the Jewish/non-Jewish divide and all the other social boundaries listed.

There is a flip side to this insightful approach to how memory is worked into the fabric of our everyday life. Its very flexibility makes it very hard to be highly specific about how musical *lieux de memoire* actually do their work. It is for this reason that I introduced the personal profiles before moving to the theoretical high ground of Pierre Nora. In the case of heritage systems, individual quests often create the *lieux de memoire* as much as do larger communal efforts. Consider the initiative of the Mexican-American singer-songwriter Tish Hinojosa, who has created a body of work she labels "Frontejas," combining the words for "border" and "Texas." You might think that with the huge population of Mexican origin and the great quantity of available music of earlier times, she would not feel the need to jump over the decades in search of meaning the way klezmer activists do. Yet her liner notes for the 1994 album *Frontejas* (Rounder CD 3132) she describes how the search for a song her mother sang led her only accidentally to the father of Mexican-American studies, Americo Paredes, who opened the doors of history and music to her. She even includes a song she wrote in *corrido* narrative form, designed to celebrate heroes, about Professor Paredes, an intellectual roots hero. Summarizing her credo, she defines her work as "a sound, a language, a feeling, a place formed by the river of culture and time washing over those who contemplate and investigate. We are all pebbles shaping the current that creates tomorrow." Her statement nicely couples the more passive "heritage" sense of past times "washing over those who contemplate" with the more active, interventionist feeling of "shaping the current." Her recording is in itself a *lieu de memoire*.

But an individual musician's motivations do not reveal much about listener desire and fulfillment, except through the indirect method of marketing strategies. Since klezmer is not as seriously commodified or tracked by the media as African-American or Mexican-American musics, statistical backup is not available. At the very least, there must be audience clusters: groups of a certain generation, class, or place that have a stake in this form of musical expression. Before citing the more familiar terrain of recent American-Jewish community building and enthusiastic reaffiliation moments, let me use the more ambiguous example of my short foray into the Berlin klezmer world, often cited as the hottest in Europe. Germany offers a very charged space for klezmer, as well as an ideal field for studying its transnational transmission. Work under way by Rita Ottens and others will give us a substantial sense of this account; here I want to present Germany merely as a knot of motivations, many strands becoming entangled temporarily as they cross and tighten under cultural pressure. I will start with impressions, then move to longer accounts by participants.

A high school teacher related how she uses the expressive forms of Eastern European Jewish culture (with klezmer high on the list) to orient her students to the very vexed issue of the place of Jews in contemporary German life. Indeed, it is hard to pick up a German newspaper (I looked at the *Berliner Tageszeitung* and the *Frankfurter Allgemeiner Zeitung*) and not encounter an article about the resettlement of new Jewish immigrants from Eastern Europe or the wrangling over forms of representation of Jewish history (memorials, museums). Some high school students will try out one of Berlin's many weekly klezmer-related concerts. There they will run into other young people who are part of a hip, world-music-conscious set that keeps its antennae tuned for new musical stimuli. Meanwhile, the older, more affluent concertgoers will flock to the sold-out concerts of Giora Feidman, the veteran Israeli klezmer guru who first recognized the German market. He is said to offer a sense of absolution and a healthy dose of New Age feel-good rhetoric at high prices to graying German audiences in upscale venues like the Philharmonic. I was told about his expensive workshops, where he did more talking about the universal spirituality of klezmer than demonstrating the playing techniques some people had come to learn (for Feidman's influence, see Kirshenblatt-Gimblett 1998b/2000:72).

Clouds of ambiguity hover around German klezmer. The many non-Jewish bands themselves take many different positions, sometimes seemingly simultaneously, on the issue of just what is being evoked. La'om, a young band consisting mostly of East Berliners, summarizes their stance this way:

> It is difficult to explain why klezmer music finds such a resonance in Germany. During a visit to America, we were often confronted by Jews curious about this. They would ask us, "Is it because Germans

have a bad conscience about the past?" The reason we play klezmer music is because we enjoy it. And we also like to think that our audience listens to us because they enjoy it and not to compensate for the bad consciences. To do otherwise serves neither the music, nor the attempt to come to terms with the German-Jewish history. (La'om 1997)

Another way to approach European motivation is to interview the Americans who travel or even live there. Judy Bressler of the Klezmer Conservatory Band has the outlook of an infrequent visitor, while Alan Bern, who lives in Berlin, philosophizes on the basis of deeper experience (quotations from my interviews of 1997–1998). Here's Bressler:

That first trip we went to Germany and Poland, we were completely wrung out, I had nightmares that whole trip, all sorts of violent dreams, basically, of decimation. We were flying home and I said to Hankus [Netsky, the bandleader], should we be coming here at all? Early on there were some bands that wouldn't go to Poland and Germany. Are we making things easier for people with guilty consciences? Are we collaborating in some way all these years later? And ultimately we decided no, these voices have not been completely stilled, and going back and doing this music there is in some minuscule way a vindication of all those Jewish voices that were stilled. The culture was pretty effectively destroyed, but the people still go on. Hitler didn't win. As complicated and emotionally draining and as many moral and ethical questions that arise on these kinds of trips, we decided it's okay that we're doing it, and it's something we're going to do, even though it's hard. I don't like being in Germany, and the sooner we leave, the better. Every person on the street that's elderly, I think where were they, and what were they doing? Everybody that's sixty or seventy or older, where were you, how much blood is on your hands? And there's no way of answering that.

This tells us more about Bressler's motivations than the Germans'. The relaxed, rootsy atmosphere of American klezmer concerts contrasts sharply with the confrontation she feels on every street corner in Germany. She forgrounds her normal sense of mission, of using entertainment to educate audiences about *yiddishkayt*, to the point of becoming questionable, needing resolution in the hope of achieving "vindication." When it comes to describing the Germans' response to what the Klezmer Conservatory Band offers, Bressler's sense of responsibility as an animator of crowds almost overcomes her detachment as observer:

The European audiences have a very academic approach, and I think they have a very academic interest. There's kind of an intellectual, somewhat detached, "okay, we're here now to learn about klezmer music and Yiddish and perhaps a bit about the culture and the people that produced this language and music." [In England] it's more, "oh great, let's party."

Often when I've gotten up to lead the dancing for a German crowd or a Polish crowd, it's a little scary. They're not used to dancing communally, they're not used to that whole scene, but they like it. It's obviously very stimulating for them, but they're just on the edge of being out of control. There's almost this overexuberance to get into the music. I've often thought, this is going to turn sour; someone's going to go down, they're going to pull a bunch of people down with them, there'll be broken ankles, and I spend a lot of time saying, "Nice and easy." They begin very intellectual and detached, and when you invite them up to dance, there's this transformation, almost like a cathartic release, to the music.

Despite her misgivings and anxieties, Bressler remains generous toward her central European audience:

I think the Holocaust left a hole in the fabric of those countries, of Poland, of Germany, that has not been closed and will never be closed. The young people are trying to come to grips with what happened and the implications of that, and taking the knowledge of what happened into the future and trying to make some sense of it.

Alan Bern, of the major American band Brave Old World, has lived in Berlin for several years. His position can be summarized in this short statement:

I wouldn't be happy to raise a family in Germany and don't see this as an emigration to Germany. Actually, I'm looking for a way to come back to the United States that would make sense to me, but I also don't want to lose the edge that being in Germany gives to me; being in Germany gives me an edge that I like and that I can use as an artist, but I almost never come to rest here, feel really relaxed, really at home, part of Germany, enjoying myself. I'm always a tourist here in a way. It's not like being a tourist in Italy.

As one who has spent a great deal of time and thought preparing material for German audiences, Bern can offer a more detailed account of motivation than Bressler:

[MS: What does Brave Old World offer the German audience?] I'm not sure; it's harder for me to be analytical about that . . . there's a cynical answer or a generous answer to that; both are guesses. The cynical one is that there's an association between Jews and culture, in the sense of high culture, and so Brave Old World carries some of that association, so there are people they call *Bildungsbürgertum* [educated middle class] who come because of that, because they have the feeling that somehow having contact with us, contact with *gebildete* interesting culture, is refined . . . that side that's missing from German culture. There are some people who come because it's klezmer music for all the good and bad reasons that people come to klezmer music . . . . From the generous point of view, I think we really are cultured, and that in fact there's stuff going on in our music that's both at the level of tap your feet to it and sway your body to it and also think hard about it.

For Bern and Brave Old World, just getting audiences into cathartic dancing is not enough. They do not spend much time explaining *yiddishkayt* to their audiences, preferring to construct complex pieces that force listeners to come up with thoughtful responses of their own. They tend to be skeptical about the ability of Germans to extract much cultural value from standard Jewish-American entertainment:

> If you're an insider, and you hear the nine thousandth performance of "Romania Romania" [a classic Jewish-American theater song that is one of Judy Bressler's standbys], that does something for you. But the Germans aren't insiders, so "Romania Romania" is to them whatever it is on its surface. They're not reminded of any history when they hear that, and that history is what provides the depth that counterbalances the superficial appearance. The whole thing comes down to "Oh, typically American, Hollywood show."

Both Bressler's and Bern's accounts suggest the layered response pattern one might expect from klezmer concertgoers in Germany, including the coupling of the superficial and the neurotic, the differential reaction according to generation and class, and the European reaction to things American.

I have offered a sketchy account of certain aspects of a very multitrack system of Jewish music representation in Germany. To go further would require a deeper history of pre-klezmer Jewish music initiatives, going back to the 1950s. The distinction between East and West German experiences would be crucial, most strongly in the last decade, when suddenly those two streams of consciousness about Jewish culture began to flow in the same social and civic channels (Rebling 1995). The point here is the clustering of motivational urges. Unlike the purely target market approach of major mediated musical forms, heritage systems like klezmer tie more tightly to the immediate needs of individuals, social "neighborhoods" and communities. They lock on to local histories, discourses about the peoples the music represents, gut responses to the cultural codes embedded in the voices and rhythms. Bressler eloquently evokes the way in which musics accidentally encountered and academically preconceived can literally take over listeners' bodies, moving them, marionette-like, to twitch and dance on the edge of danger.

Far beyond Germany, the farthest removed band I have heard came from Samara (formerly Kuibishev), a grubby Volga city in the depths of Russia. In 1993 the Samara ensemble was largely oriented toward playing classical music of Jewish origin or affiliation, but it also tipped its hat to Israeli and klezmer music. The band members, almost completely non-Jews, cited two main, mundane motivations, both pleasurable, which came as a surprise given the Western media coverage about rampant anti-Semitism in the former Soviet Union. First, they were very glad to get away from their tedious duties in the Samara Philharmonic, and second, they really enjoyed getting on a bus and touring, a rare chance to see the country and meet interesting people. For the group's organizer, a Jewish cellist, there seemed to be more at stake.

The klezmer story plays differently in the United States, where there are large, entrenched, long-term Jewish communities that exercise their taste using cozy or contested in-group discourses. There, klezmer is just one small statement within a volatile, emerging reformulation of American Jewishness. Excited over being allowed entry to prestigious universities around 1960, by 1997 Orthodox Jewish students were suing Yale University for making them live a type of dormitory life they find religiously unacceptable. This confidence of the assimilated emerges strikingly in a new penchant for proselytizing, well detailed in a *New York Times* piece by Gustav Niebuhr (May 27, 1998): "These days, some rabbis and Jewish officials . . . are actively reaching out as never before with widespread advertising in secular mainstream media and large public lectures." As the cover of *New York* magazine (February 28, 2000) puts it, "as spiritual seekers shop for faith, feel-good Judaism is becoming a big seller—even to the goyim [non-Jews]." Inside, the feature story has a photograph of a new-wave klezmer band playing to a mixed audience on Manhattan's new hot upper West Side ethnic clubhouse, Makor. But Jews, as quintessential Americans, shop for synagogues and spirituality within the bounds of their national-ethnic-religious boundaries. It's a process that began to explode in the 1960s, and it is hard to stop at the borders, even internationally, as the opening of the Saatchi synagogue in London shows. The Saatchi brothers, giants of the advertising industry, have chosen to commemorate themselves by opening a new synagogue which, fittingly, has been heralded by a gigantic advertising campaign: "At the moment, London's Underground stations are plastered with large posters selling the temple's offbeat approach to worship . . . using some of Judaism's more appealing cultural trappings—food and wine, mainly—to lure Jews back to the fold . . . current ads feature images of roast chicken . . . and promise easy-to-swallow services for an upwardly mobile, professional clientele" (*New York Times*, October 25, 1998). Doubtless, klezmer music will appear at the Saatchi services.

Unlike the novelty effect needed in London, in the aisles of the cultural supermarket that is Jewish America, klezmer has had two decades to become a standard brand, a well-known form of "our" entertainment. There are now students at my university who, when asked why they are joining the klezmer band, say, "I grew up with it." This means their parents played klezmer albums, or they heard it repeatedly at a synagogue, wedding, or bar mitzvah. The music is now taken for granted and produces the usual American response: canny consumerism. Hip, young, socially conscious professionals from the upper west side of Manhattan might favor the queer-tinged, fusion style of the Klezmatics. More mainstream listeners who like a big-band sound and old-time Yiddish show tunes might favor the Klezmer Conservatory Band. Locally, communities (as detailed in the next chapter) tend to support any lesser-known band that meets the immediate needs of Winnipeg, Milwaukee, or New Orleans. College campuses are likely to have klezmer around as part of a Jewish culture and heritage support system; April 1999 saw the first intercollegiate klezmer jam session, held at Yale, with collectives from Princeton, Brown, Yale, and Wesleyan alongside the pioneering New England Conservatory band. This music offers good, clean fun. You don't have to know Hebrew, or even Yiddish, and you don't have to really know the forgotten dance steps that go with the tunes; it's affiliation through enjoyment. Even the knowledgeable students at the collegiate jam had no idea how to dance to the tunes their colleagues were playing. This cheerfully secularist motivation links Jewish-American audiences with a large mass of European listeners who have no cultural and mental background to bring to klezmer.

But I would hate to leave a discussion of klezmer's evocative resonance on a note of fun alone. Part of klezmer's distinctive core surely has to do with reconstruction, the day-to-day work of memory. The abyss of the Holocaust (*Shoah*) does make that job more than a routine, mundane micromusic-building project. Beyond the marketing, magnetism, and personality components of klezmer does indeed lie a space of rebuilding, trenchantly characterized by Dana Villa in his writing on Hannah Arendt's politics. Not reflecting on things Jewish, he nevertheless reaches for the word "abyss":

When the medium of remembrance—tradition—dissolves or is shattered, the only escape from the abyss of forgetfulness seems to reside in the theoretical project of aggressive, critical recovery. Excavating a tradition in ruins can, as Sheldon Wolin has observed, 'remind us of what we have lost.'" (Villa 1996:8)

The leaders of the klezmer movement—if we view it as a movement and not just a scene—are often reluctant to come up with this sort of statement about their musical work. For example, this rhetoric does not emerge in the interviews cited earlier. But that does not mean there is no appreciation of the importance of "aggressive, critical recovery" among klezmer folk. A fine example of theoretical urgency arises from Hankus Netsky's reconstruction of older Philadelphia wedding music styles. There, he reassembled a group of musicians who had literally forgotten the years they spent on a bandstand, or at least found it hard to recall the tunes they had played to animate Jewish celebrants. Netsky instigated a full-scale project of remembrance which, in turn, has been enthusiastically embraced by the community.

A situation like this brings to mind the words of Yosef Yerushalmi, writing on lapses of Jewish memory: "[a] people 'forgets' when the generation that now possesses the past does not convey it to the next . . . the break in transmission can occur abruptly or by a process of erosion. A people can never 'forget' what it has never received in the first place" (Yerushalmi 1989:109). Netsky, who grew up in a klezmer family that never once took him on a wedding job, is a fine case in point. His success, and that of many others, in revitalizing the klezmer tradition suggests that behind Yerushalmi's classic statement lie a set of nuances that are not easily summarized by a simple verb like "forget."

Some klezmer searching takes musicians on a quest for the "spiritual," (a work that appears in liner notes), but cataloging the range of personal connections is much more difficult. Occasionally, responses to the music open a window into a landscape of memory, where listeners wander among the sounds in search of the past. Alicia Svigals received this e-mail communication about a piece on her solo album "Dem Trisker Rebns Khosid" (discussed later): "I have been searching the web researching Trisk Hasidim. My family were Trisker Hasidim from Kolk, Poland. All I have found so far was your album. I am going to buy it to hear this song." Intuitively, many American and European musicians realize they are creating *lieux de memoire* on a weekly basis, but this formal French term, or the bare word "evocation" I've proposed, carry only a fraction of the affective charge that the music transmits. At least for scattered listeners, if not whole audiences, another comparison comes to mind: the term *shali-*

ach tzibur, "messenger of the congregation," the characterization for the way cantors channel collective prayer toward its divine destination. Svigals's fan hopes that the violinist's re-creation, in packaged form, of a sacred-tinged tune will help satisfy his longings for the vanished world of Trisk. Of course this is a hyperbolic way of thinking about what klezmorim can do, but it provides the other end of a continuum of consciousness about the music that ranges from sheer relaxation to deep remembrance.

RECENTLY I RECEIVED AN E-MAIL from a klezmer band in Montreal that pulls together many of the issues around both motivation and overlap, allowing for a summary of those ideas. Klezmer is not a sharply mowed emerald lawn, but a meadow, mixing cultivated grasses and wildflowers, some carefully planted, some blowing across the fence, and others floating in from far away.

We start with the band's membership and function:

> My name is Marlow Bork and I am the trumpet player and a founding member of the Montreal-based Klezmer band Mazik. We have been performing together for about three years and have done many concerts, weddings, and other *simkhes* [celebrations] both here in Montreal and in Toronto. The band is made up of local professional musicians. With our full complement, our instrumentation consists of two clarinetists (B-flat, E-flat and bass, flute, piccolo), trumpet and cornet, acoustic bass and acoustic guitar.
>
> Curiously, I am the only member of the band who is Jewish, although one of the clarinet players is the chef d'orchestre of the leading Jewish wedding band in town. His knowledge of the functional as well as artistic aspects of the role of music in Jewish tradition has been invaluable. The rest of the members are well versed in myriad styles and forms. Our violinist, Alex Kehler, is one of the leading fiddlers in Montreal's Irish community as well as a fellow student in early music at McGill University. Our guitarist, Charles Gagnon, is active in the Montreal Latin and jazz scene. Our bassist, Derek Shirley, is also an accomplished jazz player, and our other clarinetist, Mark Simons, comes from a family of musicians and is also an orchestral musician with an active solo career. At McGill, I studied orchestral trumpet literature and performance, as well as the more specialized performance techniques of the natural or baroque trumpet.

We see that overlaps include not only heritage musics (here: Irish), but also jazz and the classical scene, from early music through orchestral.

Training ranges from upbringing through university schooling. The instrumentation is acoustic and "early," omitting the accordion, and covers a wide range of possibilities for arrangements. The non-Jew is the experienced, knowledgeable klezmer musician, both in terms of "functional and artistic" aspects. Here is Marlowe Bork's personal trajectory:

> I became interested in klezmer music in my first year at McGill. At the time, I was addicted to early jazz recordings from the 1920s (Louis Armstrong's Hot Fives and Hot Sevens were my introduction to this incredible music). While shopping for CDs, I came across "Harry Kandel: Master of Klezmer Music" on the Global Village label. I was curious to hear this Jewish music from the same time period, so I brought it home to give it a listen. I was hooked. Klezmer music has been my window on the world of my ancestors, and through it I became interested in Jewish history and culture.

Bork's narrative mimics the disjuncture of his experience. It starts with the musical magnetism story encountered so often for heritage musics—the accidental purchase leading to "I was hooked." A closer look shows the system of musical extensions suggested above, as Bork senses klezmer both as something totally current and as a logical expansion of his interest in a time period, the 1920s, and in acoustic music with a subcultural sound. Without warning, his account shifts to a moment of pure cultural evocation, a sudden connection to "the world of my ancestors." This turns him onto a path he had never noticed that was under his feet all the time: "I became interested in Jewish history and culture." Now he is ready to work with his colleagues to shape a band aesthetic described as a process that is both intellectual and emotional. It expresses itself through affect, a studied embodiment of feeling in performance practice:

> Our goal in the first few years was to explore all aspects of the tradition of performance practice of klezmer music. As early music majors, Alex and I have strived to maintain a certain level of authenticity as we understand it in the context of the available recordings of the first generation of klezmorim in America. However, we are also aware that any attempt at authenticity must be made with an understanding of the limitations of our ability as musicians functioning in the late twentieth century, with recordings as our only source to arrive at a true klezmer sound.
>
> We quickly learned that klezmer is a vibrant and current tradition, that we were not klezmorim from a shtetl in the Pale, and that anything we did would also reflect our biases and personal tastes. We

eventually arrived at our current and simple philosophy: start with the melody and see where it leads, let our sound develop naturally, but always keep in mind the heritage and lineage of the music. Our innovations tend therefore to be subtle. Our harmonic language is slightly more modern, and we have an eccentric approach to melodic counterpoint. The instrumental tunes from Beregovski's collection [their entire album is devoted to this repertoire] led us in many fascinating directions; some of the tunes are nostalgic, while others have a decidedly more modern sound. (Electronic communication, May 27, 1998)

Marlow and Alex offer a self-conscious critique, a very modest manifesto based on their sense of being newcomers, but with full confidence; they are not interlopers. They crave but distrust "authenticity" as they bring to klezmer the concerns of the early music work that is their academic focus. They claim always to simply "start with the melody and see where it leads," as if the music, working through their agency, could directly channel its own evolution toward a sound that unfolds "naturally," even as they recognize they are innovating in a way that might actually lead to an "eccentric approach." Particularly piquant is their projection of this stance backward, seeing in Beregovski's field collections of the 1930s a combination of the "nostalgic" and the "modern." Bork's description foreshadows what I will say about style later: that it both flows from and shapes players' philosophy. Taken as a whole, this concise and articulate account from Canada probably represents many similar histories of engagement and reflection, a voice in the transatlantic klezmer chorus.

"KLEZMER," A SHIFTING, MULTILAYERED assemblage of contexts and items, exists because many people have a stake in it for a huge variety of reasons, often several at once. In this chapter I have tried to specify those reasons, or at least large categories of motivation, grounding them in social factors that range from the crassest search for markets through the broadest structures of feeling, to use Raymond Williams's elegant term.

We can identify the channels by which a set of motivations can flow into a coherent musical praxis, combining the canonical set of early recordings, the emerging canon produced by established bands, the wisdom of experienced local musicians, and the linkages created by the expanding klezmer camps and touring networks. Starting with a motivational impulse, individuals orient themselves as players and listeners within this system. In this way klezmer is no different from other heritage musics or niche musics within the popular world. Once the music finds this kind of comfortable home, anyone can move into it with no mental baggage, a light conceptual backpack, or heavy trunks of memory, can find the right size room on the appropriate floor, and can decorate it according to taste. The range of feelings and knowledge about klezmer laid out in just the few pages of this chapter should give some sense of how roomy such musical homes can be in contemporary world music neighborhoods. Next, we need to move into those subdivisions to see how people create klezmer communities.

4

Klezmer as Community

The evidence we have about the beginning of professional Ashkenazic instrumental musicians—when a klezmer was still a *spielmann,* deep in the German lands hundreds of years ago—is all about communities. Town records talk about competition between Jewish and Christian entertainers. Bands were local and fierce and seemed to need constant patrolling by the burgher-bureaucrats bent on propriety and fair business practices (see Salmen 1991 for a survey).

When the Jews are noticed in the Russian Empire, the musicians turn up in the tax records as part of the organization of urban life. Moshe Beregovski (1892–1961), the pioneering ethnomusicologist who contributed immeasurably more to our knowledge of klezmer life and music than anyone else, collected some hard data. In 1794–1795 there were two klezmorim in the Belorussian town of Smilovichi, inhabited by 53 Jewish families, and there was only one in Pogost, home to 82 Jewish men and 133 Jewish women. In 1811 Bragin (Rechitsa district) could boast of two klezmorim among 259 Jews, and Kletsk (Slutsk district) of three professional musicians among 662 Jews. Well, concludes Beregovski, projecting these figures across the vast geography of the Pale of Settlement, there must have been thousands of klezmorim in a continuous chain of overlapping musical and family links in a spread-out system of town-based musical professionalism.

These urban entertainers came from tight hereditary circles and spoke their own argot (Rothstein 1998/2000). Their portraits in famous works of fiction like Sholom Aleichem's novel *Stempenyu* offer a combination of heartthrob violinists and workmanlike backup bands. Although *Stempenyu* might look to us today as somewhat romantically exaggerated portrait of a musician, its author did spend considerable time with a klezmer family and he offers telling ethnographic detail. Anyone who takes the trouble to footnote the musicians' vocabulary can't be completely unreliable as a witness to the klezmer lifestyle.

By 1900, Beregovski tells us, the music bug had become contagious. Amateur musicians studied with local klezmer teachers, learning the violin, less frequently the clarinet or flute. These enthusiasts—almost always men, except among middle-class families in the big cities—played solo or accompanied family singing. Upward mobility struck the klezmorim themselves; they wrote away for classical etudes to gentrify their fiddling. Their sons moved into the emerging Russian conservatories as soon as Jews were allowed access to higher-class musicianship and career hopes, in the last quarter of the nineteenth century. Before long, a figure like Mischa Elman (1891–1967), from a klezmer lineage, could become an international virtuoso and recording artist. But even as far back as the 1830s, before his early death, Mikhail Guzikov had toured Europe as an eastern klezmer star, impressing no less a listener than Felix Mendelssohn. Klezmorim, in short, were city-minded musical ambassadors, carrying tunes and styles across a vast network of Jewish culture that stretched from the Ottoman borderlands to the bourgeois bulwarks of central Europe. They combined the restlessness and spiritual spark of a *dybbuk* (a displaced soul seeking a body) with the cozy, gossipy communality of traditional small-town and emerging big-city Jewish life.

This pattern of social organization spilled over to the United States during the construction of a transatlantic Eastern European Jewish community life as part of the great wave of immigration of the 1880s–1920s. Klezmorim recorded dozens of exuberant recordings in New York that set the tone for stylistic evolution everywhere. Until very recently, our view of American klezmer history has been blocked by the musical mountain of this recorded repertoire. It has kept us from seeing many musical landmarks and landscapes that lay beyond New York, in "the provinces" (*di provints*), not only on the eastern seaboard, but in smaller, faraway places like Milwaukee. Research by Hankus Netsky, as noted earlier both seminal modern bandleader and ethnomusicologist, is putting things in focus. In Netsky's hometown, Philadelphia, so near yet so far from New York, a tightly organized, durable klezmer scene closely mirrored the European world Beregovski sought to reclaim, and at the same time period; Netsky has manuscript tunebooks from as far back as 1910.

In Philadelphia, klezmer families ruled the roost and kept their ties to their cities of origin through the *landsmanshaftn,* locality-based social organizations. These cliques of immigrants stayed true to the cities they had left behind by gathering periodically and offering social support to members. The direct carryover of musical taste, a surprising finding for the supposedly homogenizing world of American immigrants, klezmorim strengthened the culture of Philadelphia's ex-Teplekers, Kriovozerites, Kievans, Kishinevers, and Briskites. As in Eastern Europe, family ties were strong, but so were ties to non-Jewish colleagues. In Europe, this meant links to Roma ("gypsy") colleagues, while in Philadelphia, Italians filtered into the klezmer scene. Also European was the drive toward upward mobility, meaning that a prominent musician such as Jacob "Jakie" Hoffman could fulfill his musical ambitions by working with prestige organizations like the orchestra of the Ballets Russe and the Philadelphia Orchestra, while Harry Kandel could land well-regarded parallel jobs such as assistant band director for the great John Philip Sousa.

The Philadelphia repertoire is distinctive. Local klezmorim could not play weddings using the standard tunebook of New York musicians, since local custom prevailed, despite the short distance and the overwhelming power of New York's Jewish presence. Items as basic to the experience of a Jewish wedding as the *patsh-tants* ("clapping dance") or the required "good night waltz" at the end of the long celebration differed from city to city. The same is true for Boston and Milwaukee, according to Netsky, in terms of both the site-specific nature of the repertoire and the sociomusical power that resided in just a few families or individuals from specific European places (Hankus Netsky, interviews, 1997–1998).

In Jewish-American communities in the first half of the twentieth century, *simkhe* ("celebration") tended to be centralized in the catering hall. In Philadelphia, Uhr's was such a prominent locus of activity that the streetcar would unload guests in front of the hall rather than at the regular stop. In Newark, New Jersey, a smaller settlement, the Lipschitz family had a near monopoly on local festivities, as remembered by Melvin Strauss. Strauss, later an eminent orchestral conductor, spent the years of his youth (1947–1960) playing both for the Lipschitzes and for the extension of local Jewish music-making in the Catskills during the summer. In a 1998 interview, Strauss reflected on the scene:

> The Schary Family Manor was sold to the family I worked for and I think that must have happened about the early forties, maybe the late thirties, and the name was changed to Clinton Manor. The place became rather posh, sort of pseudo-Hollywood in decor, and very active. The mother ran the place . . . the sons, one became the caterer, another became the florist. I worked for the one who was in my estimation a true klezmer, Herbie Lipschitz.
>
> Herbie Lipschitz had enough sense to know his name had to be changed to get enough business outside of the Manor, and so he became known as Herb Larson and his band; it was a small band, usually four or five of us. Herbie was the clarinet and alto sax player, I was the pianist, we had a bass player who also played the violin a lit-

tle bit, and the trumpet player and the drummer. These other people all had full-time jobs in order to support themselves during the day; I was a full-time student. The bass player was a full-time exterminator of rodents and bugs . . . the trumpet player was a pot and pan seller. He was the only non-Jew, an Italian, and he worked very hard to support his large family. The drummer was a pharmaceutical supply salesman who thought he was Frank Sinatra; he not only played the drums but sang pop tunes.

The infiltration of Italians, characteristic of Philadelphia, holds for Newark and presumably much of the northeastern United States, as does the tight family business control. Clinton Manor might have made a special contribution to American culture being the likely model for the catering hall in the 1959 novel *Goodbye, Columbus*, since Philip Roth was from Newark. Strauss thinks that the wedding setting of the 1969 film version of the novel might even have been modeled on Clinton Manor, since it so closely matches his memory of the place.

Strauss's description of events and repertoire offers an accurate if perhaps jaundiced view, by a future classical musician, of the Newark scene of his day:

> I played in Clinton Manor every weekend, with at least one affair Saturday evening; sometimes there were simultaneous affairs, two or three weddings or parties going on in the same building, and always Sunday an afternoon and an evening wedding. All of this was handled with the greatest efficiency by the Lipschitz family, but not always with the greatest scruples [for example, they reused flowers for two events while billing both customers].
>
> The repertoire we played was a combination of so-to-speak Jewish music, Jewish Russian, Jewish Polish, that is, and American pop, with a tiny invasion of Latin American. The Jewish music consisted of Russian *shers* and *freylekhs* [standard fare in Europe as well]. It was entirely improvised, and Herbie Lipschitz was very good at this and very, very loud, putting the bell of his clarinet next to the microphone as close as was humanly possible and blasting everybody out of the place to the point where the people who attended the parties could not talk to each other. But they did not seem to mind; everybody had a good time and the high level of musical volume seemed to contribute to that.

Philip Roth's account, while sparse in describing the music-making at the posh Newark wedding he so lovingly describes in *Goodbye, Columbus,* corroborates Strauss's and Netsky's description on a couple of points. For example, Neil, the narrator, notes that "the band was playing between courses." We know that caterers ruled the roost and absolutely forbade musicians to play while food was being served. Indeed, Neil notes that "Brenda and I danced closely, and we only sat down when the waiters began to circulate with the main course."

Three other small descriptive passages offer more of Roth's ethnography of the Newark catering hall: (1) "Up on the stage, Harry Winters (nee Weinberg) was leading his band in a medley from *My Fair Lady*; on the floor, all ages, all sizes, all shapes were dancing." (2) "Rose and Pearl did the Charleston with one another (while their husbands examined woodwork and chandeliers)"; (3) "Near the end of the evening, Brenda . . . did a Rita Hayworth tango with herself" (Roth 1959:109–10).

The Weinberg-to-Winters name change rings true. So does the mini-catalogue of repertoire: a brief survey of American styles—Broadway musical, vintage dances for the older folks—and the "Latin invasion" mentioned by Strauss and all subsequent sources on the Jewish wedding. By the late 1940s, musicians who couldn't handle this range of American and Latin styles couldn't find work or were regarded as throwbacks. Brenda seems to be inspired by what Strauss calls the catering hall's "posh, neo-Hollywood" decor to come up with her own movie-inspired moves. The "all ages, all sizes, all shapes" line confirms Strauss's view from the piano bench that everybody had a good time at Clinton Manor.

Conspicuously absent in Roth's account are the *sher* and the *freylekhs*, the basic dance tunes of the Eastern European Jewish wedding. One suspects this omission is due to the novel's strong interest in setting off Brenda's wealthy, suburban, Americanized family from Neil's lower middle-class, inner-city, Yiddish-inflected home. Thus by the 1950s we no longer have the unitary American klezmer city, but rather a set of class and generational musical choices and fashion statements that complicate the local scene. By the time of the 1969 film version of *Goodbye, Columbus*, a further layer of subtle observation supplements Roth's accurate description: in the movie, the wedding band throws in two Israeli-identified numbers for the eager and animated guests.

The thoroughgoing Americanization that overtook Philip Roth's Newark is the most benign version of a pattern of radical disjuncture that includes the extremes of Stalinism and Nazism. Though it may seem strange to lump suburbanization/assimilation with cultural repression and outright genocide, a whole set of historical factors converged to reshape the klezmer's tie to his community in the 1940s. Even in the comfort of Netsky's Philadelphia, the hereditary klezmer families edged out of the business, leaving memories in the attic—literally—that he could find when he matured as a musician. His immediate family members had refused to immerse him in a music they found beneath his potential level of musicianship, outside the range of acceptable professionalism. Tellingly, his mother pointed to the bandleader for the Academy Awards show as a possible model rather than to the classical music virtuosi that earlier generations had seen as a model alternative to klezmerhood. The phantom city of the TV set superseded the real-life community that a musician might animate. Netsky's family history supports the pattern of "rupture and recovery" that Kirshenblatt-Gimblett (1998b:65) describes as the basic trajectory of American klezmer. But it is perhaps an overstatement to say that "the decades immediately preceding the klezmer revival are generally viewed as a wasteland" (ibid.). Some of the repertoire survived in the *simkhe* celebration context and the small-label LP recordings of the 1950s and 1960s. The gap was relatively short and the scene was quick to recover, especially in comparison with the European context of annihilation and suppression.

For European musicians who survived Stalin and Hitler, few were in a position to offer cultural continuity through klezmer. In the USSR, Soviet forms of music-making, especially the variety-show formats called *estrada*, standardized acceptable ethnic entertainment, and this standard has continued in post-Soviet times in Russia/Ukraine and among Russian immigrant communities in American cities. Occasionally, skilled klezmer-style musicians do emerge from the post-Soviet lands, as witnessed by their inclusion in the late-1990s Festival of Jewish Traditions from the Former Soviet Union created by New York's Center for Traditional Music and Dance (CTMD). But the need for an outside sponsoring agency to stage such a festival shows that klezmer-style music is not being naturally supported within the emigre community. The CTMD offers regular Sunday sessions of traditional music to bolster interest in older traditional instrumental and vocal styles of the Yiddish tradition.

Given this picture of ruin and rechanneling, when we try to reestablish how the klezmer system intersects with community life from the 1970s to 2000, we have to appeal to different theoretical models than classic ethnography and to consider more complex contexts. As ethnomusicologists continually stress in their work, moments of performance by themselves create communities of listeners by trapping them in a web of songs, sound colors, and the simple ritual of gathering together for a common purpose that often combines music with dance. The best descriptions of performance moments also suggest how music events create time capsules. These space-time simultaneities have been articulated in cultural theory by means of Bakhtin's concept of chronotope. Perhaps almost overused in its original terrain of literary studies, chronotope has hardly been deployed by ethnomusicologists for describing what happens when a gathered group meets music head-on. The term offers a possibility of crystalizing the very diverse and contested ways that "klezmer" has become reinserted or has infiltrated into Jewish and non-Jewish life in recent decades.

Bakhtin tells us that a chronotope specifies a fused sense of time and space, and to the chronotope "belongs the meaning that shapes narrative" (Morson and Emerson 1990:368, 371). In short, to suggest a chronotope means specifying a time-place nexus that helps us understand how people make sense—make narrative—of the multiple contexts that they embody and experience. As Bakhtin says, "local folklore interprets and saturates space with time, and draws it into history." Nothing could be truer about the way klezmer has been domesticated into numerous ways of life in hundreds of cities of the Euro-American world (with expected offshoots in places like Australia). The proliferation of recordings has meant that eventually everyone can hear each other, but local understandings of what "klezmer" might be still dictate the way the music is heard, played, and understood. Any occurrence of klezmer creates a chronotope, a cohesive feeling about place and time that tends to assimilate the immediate moment to larger patterns of local knowledge.

Chronotopes can also be transferable, universal, the obvious case here being *Fiddler on the Roof*. Its standardized "shtetl" portrait relies heavily on the atmosphere of music, especially including notions of "tradition" as linked to "the fiddler." This off-the-shelf chronotope is available in every society's household, as witnessed by productions of *Fiddler* in Japan and India. It is a dependable kitchen tool for domesticating the "klezmer" concept. The shtetl chronotope helped in the transition from popular culture images of musical *yiddishkayt* (homy Jewishness) to community-based cultural production. While a product like *Fiddler* presents a simple chronotope, today's klezmer world offers many varieties of space-time-sound fusions that almost beg for an extra term—sonochronotope?

Some examples might sketch out the scope of possible future analysis, including both the American and the European contexts in which klezmer now operates as a significant marker of meaning. I'll begin with two very different American klezmer chronotopes, one nomadic and one sedentary.

1997: I am sitting at the Knitting Factory in New York, a chic club that specializes in avant-garde jazz, world music, and performance art. I am listening to the Klezmatics, a major American band that tours Europe and is currently influential in Italy. To my right sits a lady in her seventies, a native Yiddish speaker, who ignores the more radical, contemporary aspects of the club and the band's positioning. She likes their fluency with the Yiddish language and with what she remembers as the sound of Eastern European Jewish music. Part of the Klezmatics' chronotope links up with hers, and she is uninterested in noticing her lack of fit with the group's attitude, such as their suggestion of homosexuality and drug use as possible ingredients of a postmodern klezmerism.

To my left sits a six-year-old boy who is very excited about hearing the Klezmatics live. I ask him what he likes best, and he says, "Their first album." Born in 1991, the year of that first album, the boy is experiencing a heightened version of the marketed chronotope, the artifact of the group condensed into a set of processed sound-objects in the defined but indeterminate space-time of the studio.

The band itself inhabits and spins off multiple chronotopes when it plays. They are "here," but their music-making draws on countless musical space-time frameworks, just a few of which, for one band member, were suggested by the remarks of Alicia Svigals in the last chapter; expanding the list for all the Klezmatics would include teenage metal band rehearsals, recitals at the New England Conservatory, Latin jazz gigs in New York clubs, playing on the streets of Paris with Minorcan musicians—just for starters. The collective number of memory moments that shape tonight's chronotope is staggering. "Klezmer" here and now offers an overlap, a meeting point among the band members and with the audience that helps shape a space-time nexus located temporarily in the Knitting Factory.

What do the Klezmatics have to say about its collective chronotope? Let us return to Alicia Svigals, founding member, violinist, and an articulate spokesperson for the group:

I think what we do is a very New York City music aesthetic . . . it's clangy, it's noisy, it's postindustrial, related to what they call the downtown music scene, you know, the lower east side music crowd that kind of centers around the Knitting Factory, the new music scene. . . .

I guess even though . . . music gets out there everywhere, we all still live in a place, and musicians who play together cluster in groups and come up with a style, and that's sort of what happens here.

So there is a sound, this noise sound, this downtown New York noise sound that people think—and I would agree—reflects the ambience here in the streets.

We live here, and we make music here, both in the sense of the jackhammers outside my window, also here in the sense that we're part of a musical school. Not to mention the uptown hip-hop, everything that's happening in contemporary music, and then it goes everywhere. We live here, we make the music here, we are New Yorkers, and then it goes everywhere, whether it's via our recordings or via us touring, it's the same.

[MS: So you're carrying the city with you, the city is kind of portable.] Yeah, yeah. Earlier on in our career we would play differently for different audiences than we do now. In particular, we had some out noisy stuff we would not play for predominantly older audiences . . . we did a week in Century Village, it was clear we should not do our most way-out music there, and we did trad stuff we wouldn't have bunched together in one program. But now we've sort of come to a point where we really do the same program everywhere in terms of the actual numbers that are on the set list, but how we play them can vary. (Interview, 1998)

When pressed, Svigals came up with examples of more than casual differences among gigs, but she is absolutely right about the overall sensibility at work, since staid Germans and novice Italians pick up on it as much as knowing, gay San Franciscans: the Klezmatics have a profile that does say "New York City with attitude," a chronotope that combines that place with this time, the 1990s. Sometimes bands outlive or outwear these time-space packages, or listeners extend them in countless ways. For example, I was told in Germany in 1997 that two American independent films shot in Brooklyn (*Smoke* and *Blue in the Face*) were understood by certain hip young Germans to be within the chronotope of the Klezmatics, and that when some of them actually went to Brooklyn in search of this nexus, they were disappointed.

All I mean to say here is that when people gather in a public space or around their loudspeakers at home, they are certainly here, but that here is an overlay of chronotopes: in the living room but in the shtetl, or in the Knitting Factory but perhaps also in New Jersey fifty years ago. This understanding of movable chronotopes is accentuated by a band like the Klezmatics, who both tour and record very successfully. They also scatter chronotopes in their work, referencing multiple worlds in a single piece, as in their version of Naftule Brandwein's 1926 "Fun tashlikh," which starts with raucous Balkan-Middle Easternisms (including Arabic ululations) and shifts into Jewish dance-tune gear, moving listeners from one time-space frame to another. To cite Bakhtin again: "Chronotopes are mutually inclusive, they coexist, they may be interwoven with, replace or oppose one another, contradict one another or find themselves in ever more complex interrelationships" (426). The klezmer world offers rich possibilities for this sort of animated play of meanings and identifications.

The Klezmatics example illustrates the notion of a nomadic klezmer community, one model of klezmer urbanity. Like all nomads bringing goods to market, klezmorim have strategies, as Svigals only reluctantly suggests. Judy Bressler, vocalist for the very durable Klezmer Conservatory Band, can fill us in more on the local adjustments that groups make deliberately over twenty years. It is particularly her role as singer that is crucial, since she carries the textual meanings that offer an audience more than the surface thrill of textural timbres and a foot-stomping beat:

> Is it a Jewish audience? Getting a yes doesn't necessarily tell me much; what that really means, we don't know. But I'll assume if it's a Jewish audience they're going to get something, even if they're secular Jews, which odds are, they're going to be. . . . I'm going to assume they'll know what a *dreydl* is [the Chanukah toy], what a *bris* is [a circumcision]. A non-Jewish audience may not even know what a *shul* is [a synagogue], let alone a cantor. In terms of the introductions, which words I'm using, in terms of the tunes we're picking out. We might choose songs with fewer lyrics, simpler lyrics, something with a more repetitive chorus, so that people aren't overwhelmed by all of this language.
>
> [MS: Like what?] Like "Odessa Mama"—that's a lot of language. The chorus repeats, but that's a long story, there's three long verses with a lot of language. If we're playing out in the middle of the country, we may choose not do that; we might do "Makhetyneste mayne," which is shorter, fewer language, and people can relate to the theme of that more universally: we're getting married, and everybody's getting uptight, the two families are getting on each other's nerves—everybody can get into that, as opposed to a song that's about—Odessa; they never heard of Odessa? What's Odessa? Where's Odessa? So what? So that kind of stuff, we'll tailor the program according to the crowd.
>
> If it's a very elderly crowd, they're going to want to hear certain chestnuts, so we'll try to do some old favorites. How many children are there? How many young people in the crowd? We'll try to psych it out before we start the program by talking to the sponsor to try and get a feel for it, or if we can't get that information ahead of time, then when we get there, we're scurrying around trying to get that—oh, you've got six groups coming from different synagogues.
>
> [MS: Why would non-Jewish people hire the band?] Cross-cultural enrichment, multicultural exploration. Colleges and universities, churches; every now and then we get hired by church groups, or Christian institutions of learning, high schools or colleges, or regular concert series—world music.

Bressler's narrative, like Svigals's, relies on the sense of a strong, even stubborn band profile. Contrast this construct with the shape-shifting of the Moroccan band described by Philip Schuyler (1984), conciliatory commercial nomads who move from the streets to parties to a recording studio. There is less carryover, less stability in the overall profile than for the

Klezmatics or the KCB. American society is less stratified than Moroccan and more uniform in its sense of how musical chronotopes fit into middle-class lifestyles.

This stability allows for the development of a sedentary klezmer community, an almost bourgeois embodiment of what was once a semipariah profession. One such community exists, and more have been proliferating lately on the model of the oldest and most durable settlement, called KlezKamp. Since 1985, a five-day workshop held annually at a run-down hotel in the Catskill Mountains has anchored the notion of klezmer community by actually creating one. Henry Sapoznik, KlezKamp's founder and still its director, gives some background:

> The prototype was the fact that I had taught at camps that were teaching Appalachian music, I had gone to Balkan camp, and saw those. . . . The thing that was a little disconcerting is that [the Balkan camp] was run by people who were not members of the community. It was mostly Jews who ran it, and they were reductions of the culture, so they treated that culture as a sort of smorgasbord. Okay, we're going to take out the music and the songs and the dance, and that's pretty much it, and the rest of the culture doesn't interest us. Which I felt was sort of disingenuous, because the stuff isn't out of context. You can't do the songs without the language, the literature, reduce all these poetic images and stuff, just teach people to mouth the words.
>
> I was concerned that people get on stage and even if they can play a tune they end up offering this weird context for their audiences. People come away less enlightened than they think they are. . . . [He was aiming at] recontextualization—try as much as possible to have people with a high degree of cultural literacy, to bring the context into the tune. (Interview, 1996)

Sapoznik is suggesting a notion of comprehensive community that goes beyond the other American heritage-music models—Appalachian, Balkan—he had been involved in, and it is in this way that KlezKamp seems urban: not just one artistic-cultural ghetto but a set of neighborhoods. So he was pleased when older people joined in:

> What started to happen was, when you had musicians coming, concentric circles started slowly moving out. The next group of people to show up were basically people who were like an older constituency. The average age of the KlezKamp population at first was in their thirties. It was a mirror of ourselves as sort of the cultural avant-garde, and as older people started hearing about it, they started constituting on the one hand a passive . . . they were the audience as such and they

represented sort of the reaction and the approval of this, but they also brought—a lot of them were not players—social context the music existed in. They would offer feedback to the younger players of the context in which the music and the song and the dance, that they experienced from growing up. So suddenly there was this other dimension . . . people would say, "I remember when this was done."

As the concentric circles widened to include families and Europeans, as well as gay/lesbian and Orthodox Jewish circles, the klezmer city became not exactly a utopia, since the factions quarreled, as in all Jewish towns, but certainly a highly viable urban enclave that re-creates and reshapes itself each Christmastime in the Catskills. For musicians like the Klezmatics (one of whom is the assistant director, while others teach), KlezKamp is a kind of place where you come home, this being a metaphor for the power of this arbitrary, sedentary city to anchor a whole transcontinental scene. Spinoff camps—there are several now in various locales internationally—offer emerging klezmer collectives, a unique and distinctive phase in a long history of urban Jewish music-making, part of both a cultural/spiritual and a marketing network:

There's a kind of continuity in the infrastructure of KlezKamp. What started as this group-specific, just us kids—hey kids, let's put on a camp; I've got a violin, I've got a room—now, as one person put it—a major band—we want to come to KlezKamp because it's the Jewish music world's trade show. Where you're seen, where you get gigs—oh, the Jewish community center of Moot Point, Michigan, we need a klezmer band. It's an imprimatur in a way.

KlezKamp is no simulacrum. It's the real thing, making a measurable difference in the crystalization of a type of community, but its absolute arbitrariness, combined with its accommodating changeability, suggests the postmodern anyway. And the "community" itself never convenes except at the camp, so we would need a word that specifies the sedentary nature of this klezmer city but also suggests the type of improvisatory yet stable collective represented here. Perhaps kaleidoscopic might work, in that the pieces—fragments of Yiddish culture—stay the same, but time turns them round and round into different patterns at KlezKamp.

While KlezKamp is kaleidoscopic, the Wholesale Klezmer Band of western Massachusetts is fixed in a milieu and is committed to supplying the glue for local celebrations week in and week out or, to put it more substantively, to year-round community building. Joe Kurland, founding member, Yiddish songwriter, and spokesperson, eloquently describes the mission of the band:

There was a need. From the very first, when we first started per-forming—did we have anything to teach people? Basically all we had was mostly my memory of what weddings were like [in Brooklyn] We saw at weddings people had no idea what to dance—I'd go out and help them dance. When people would call up and ask, "What kind of dance do you do to this?" I'd start explaining. As time went on, I learned from other sources besides my memory, so I knew more and more I could explain, and people asked more and more questions, so it became something I do. At one point as I was doing a brochure, I decided I'll write it down, and then they can think of different ques-tions to ask. . . .

When you hire the Wholesale Klezmer Band, you're also hiring someone who's going to teach you how to do a traditional wedding. Not the *khupe* part [the ceremony proper] necessarily, that's the rabbi's job, but everything else. People have called and said, "We'd like to have Jewish music, but we'd also like to have a pop band for danc-ing." I'll show you how to dance. You'll be so occupied with Jewish dancing you won't have time for other kinds of dancing. You don't need a partner, and you don't have to know what to do. . . .

There's one dance in particular we tell people about and often peo-ple who come from communities who don't know each other or don't know *yiddishkayt*—it's where we weave people. You have the khosn's [groom's] family in a line and the kale's [brides] family in a line and weave them in and out and in and out until they don't know who's who and they're all one. People really like the symbolic quality of that mixing communities. It makes people feel really included when we do that. (Interview, 1998)

The Wholesale Klezmer Band is what I've come to call a "territory band" in the tradition of jazz historians. All across the United States, local en-sembles play a vital role in their immediate social environment. They tend not to tour much, and while they produce an album or two, their record-ings tend to work more as promotional devices than as income- or tour-producing products. Kurland's group takes this role exceptionally seri-ously. In addition to Jewish celebratory events, they play for a variety of socially oriented benefits, like Bosnian/Rwandan relief or a joint event with an African-American group at an interracial community center in Boston.

Kurland is strongly drawn to the didactic bent of Yiddish folklore and folklife, so evident in the roles of the *badkhn,* the moralizing wedding en-tertainer of Eastern Europe, or the *magid,* the itinerant preacher. The band has placed a guide to the Jewish wedding on its website. As Kurland explains, if it promotes business in their territory that's fine, but if it helps someone in faraway California, that's nice too. By teaching their clients, the band builds the very community that sustains it. The principle can be extended to an extraordinary range of venues, like the party the Wholesale Klezmer Band played at a ski resort, mostly for Jews: if the mountain won't come to the band, the band can travel to the mountain. Relentlessly tracking community contexts, the band moves on many pathways in its musical mission of mixing education, pleasure, and business. We might call this situation the self-constructed klezmer community, one link in a site-specific yet loosely linked network of chronotope cousins that stretches across the American landscape.

Small towns do not necessarily breed these self-constructs, born of local bandleaders' drive to reach out to a scattered Jewish community. The Santa Cruz, California, area shares some basic demographics with Kurland's Pioneer Valley, Massachusetts, base—mostly white, middle-class, educated, counter-culture oriented—yet things work out very differently. Laurie Tanenbaum, the only Jewish and only klezmer-knowledgeable member of the local band Hoo-tza-tza, describes the ensemble's shaping process more as a free play of band members' interests than as an effort to find and shape a coherent body of ethnic listeners. She seemed surprised when I brought up this issue. Within the extremely eclectic atmosphere of Santa Cruz's cultural life, which probably has more kinds of music per capita than any small city in America, a mixed band can find a very cosmopolitan audience easily, creating a multicultural klezmer community.

> While I was getting into klezmer, getting all these recordings and transcribing, in the meantime Annie and Steve had been playing music for fun with some other people we know and had gotten hold of the Sapoznik book and the Kammen book. So they started playing tunes from these books; I'm not sure they had recordings. We were all friends, and they had gotten interested in this through their folk music interests. We had gotten together and played tunes for fun. We were doing Celtic music, some klezmer; Steve and I would do mandolin and violin early classical music duets. Very eclectic. Very Santa Cruzy.

> We played once a week for tips at this cafe, Friday nights at Espresso Royale, and Saturday at this Italian restaurant called Giovanni's, where they gave us dinner and added a little to our tip jar. [MS: where did you get the name "Hoo-tza-tza"?] We were thinking of a lot of different names; Daniel liked that rhythm yell from the song; it just seemed the best name, basically. It had a good sound; it was kind of a musical name. We were thinking of other things like "streets of the world" that we didn't pick, and I'm glad.

We were doing all those different kinds of music, and that's when we begin to say, "Oh we should make a tape," because people would ask, "Do you guys have a tape?" Then Daniel and Robin decided to quit the band. Annie and I felt really strongly we wanted to keep the band going. I played jazz with Mark, who's the bass player in the band, and I brought Mark in; it was nice to have a bass player, and I had started playing music with Ken, more a rock band kind of thing, but more Middle Eastern influenced. I brought him in, and the idea originally was that he would play guitar, but he was a lot more interested in playing percussion. He was doing drumming (very Santa Cruz), he did folk guitar, and rock guitar, and he'd taken drumming classes. He studied Middle Eastern drumming. He became a good hand drummer, and because he was studying all this Middle Eastern stuff, that kind of helped us to bring in more of the Middle Eastern aspect, and some of the Sephardic rhythms, and later on I made friends with a guy who lived here for a while who was Sephardic, and he got us into doing more of the Sephardic music, so our style as a band evolved. Now our band is more of a mix, Middle Eastern and Sephardic as well as klezmer.

Steve had suggested we focus on instrumental and the klezmer and the gypsy, less vocals, less Celtic when we reorganized the band. Now we do Eastern European and Middle Eastern dance music.

Finally, I asked Laurie about the band's needs versus the audience's interests:

> [MS: You're describing this completely in terms of what you wanted to do; didn't you have to think about what people want to hear?] I think we weren't thinking too much about the commercial aspect all along. We more were thinking of wanting to do a good job, wanting to be good. It didn't have anything to do with [finding a niche], though we did find a niche, people liked what we were doing. We didn't try to fit into a niche.

Hoo-tza-tza's context overlaps somewhat with the big-city multiculturalism suggested in an earlier chapter for the situation of a klezmer band in Vienna, where disparate band members very consciously created a band profile to tap into the small market for "world music." In both cases, there is a cosmopolitan crowd willing to look for variety, but there the resemblance ends. Leon Pollak in Vienna has to stay pretty close to a norm for "Jewish music," to find a brand-name identity, while Hoo-tza-tza can move in and out of the Jewish material at will, since apparently "Jewishness" is a neutral quantity within the music spectrum, outside of the small Santa Cruz Jewish community's patronage of the band.

The range of repertoire of territory bands usually parallels a combination of regional taste and identity seeking, on the part of both the band and their audience. In southeastern Michigan, the Klezmer Fusion Band describes their mix this way:

> Yiddish/klezmer (including folk and theater music), Israeli/Hebrew (including contemporary, folk, and dance tunes), and religious (including music from Chabad/Hasidic, liturgical, and biblical sources). Traditional ethnic and folk instruments such as the clarinet, mandolin, and acoustic guitar are backed by a rhythm section which emphasizes jazz, rock and roll, and Latin styles—hence the name "Klezmer Fusion."
>
> Some songs are original compositions in Hebrew or English. New lyrics with Jewish theme and content are added to popular rock and roll tunes. (Liner notes to Klezmer Fusion Band cassette, 1998).

In short, something for everyone, including diverse band members and a wide potential audience over a large territory.

Some additional European examples, gleaned from a short survey in 1997, will round out this survey of klezmer community types. By that time the American approach to klezmer had been available to Europeans for nearly a decade. Rippling out in concentric circles from early festival activity in a number of countries, the effect of American recordings and touring groups intensified through the 1990s, showing no signs of peaking by the end of the decade. Accelerated expansion in Italy succeeded earlier waves of German, Scandinavian, Dutch, and other activity. Not just country by country, but city by city, the profile of Jewish music-making depends heavily on local histories, personalities, and opportunities. A serious survey lies well beyond the scope of this book, so I will highlight just a couple of 1997 examples from Krakow, Bologna, and Vienna.

In Krakow, Poland, the old Jewish neighborhood called Kazimierz, a fourteenth-century suburb created by the King for the Jews, ended up as a proletarian neighborhood in the nineteenth century. Used as a ghetto by the Nazis during World War II until the Jews were transported to their death, Kazimierz today contains the only substantial surviving set of buildings and cemetery from the thousand years of Jewish history in Poland, in a city where the Jews formed 25 percent of the population in 1939. This shell of a place has become a pilgrimage site and almost a theme park for German tourist buses, diasporic Jews, and Israeli school groups, who literally rub shoulders as they try to inhale memory and manufacture meaning from the gravestones and synagogues, drawing on the evocative power of the market square or even of Steven Spielberg's film

Schindler's List, which was partially shot here. The close proximity to Auschwitz has made Kazimierz a steady stop listed on the "Jewish tour" of Orbis, the Polish national tourist agency, in a brochure available in every hotel. We are dealing with a pattern of commercialized remembrance that allows an American Jew to place an article on tracing his Polish roots in the section of the Sunday *New York Times* called "The Sophisticated Traveler."

In the almost total absence of a local Jewish population, the musicians who play in the Jewish-theme restaurants of Kazimierz create a phantom klezmer city, where the authenticity of the site overrides any questioning of the provenance of the performers and even of their musical offerings. In one week in October, a partial list included the following:

Kroke. This band was mentioned in chapter 3 as an example of marketing prowess. Their name is the Yiddish word for the city of Krakow but, oddly enough, they resonate little with the locale of their birth and band origins. They avoid both a local sound and an American klezmer approach, trying instead to universalize the resonance of Kazimierz in some indefinable way while gesturing toward Jewishness. As was mentioned earlier, they were rewarded with a contract with WOMAD in England for international world music representation. At some level they represent a vanished Krakow community they partly manifest through two band members' recent discovery of Jewish family background, but here we have perhaps the most extremely attenuated notion of "community" one can imagine. Kroke is not alone; the next examples of Krakowian musicians are even more problematic from this point of view.

Olga. Having grown up in Switzerland, this young, vivacious Krakowian blonde heard American klezmer cassettes her father played and decided to earn some money singing in Kazimierz when she came home for college. She says that Schwyzerdütsch ("Swiss German") is close to Yiddish, facilitating her crossover into Jewish territory.

Russian gypsy band. These young non-Jewish expatriates from the East, classically trained, have found they can offer the old "gypsy" cabaret repertoire in Kazimierz's Ariel Cafe.

Irina Urbanska and Ladislaw Leitz. This duo appear in Kazimierz and abroad—from Germany to Canada—as representatives of "Polish Jewish" music. For example, in 1997 they acted as ambassadors to a week-long gathering in a German city, where emerging Polish–German links demand some representation of culture and community. Along with a Polish early music group and a standardized "village" ensemble, Urbanska and Leitz represented Polish-Jewish culture. Yet neither is Jewish. The two Poles, about 70 years old, are retired musicians of the classical, operetta, and jazz scene in Krakow. Irina, a soprano, has learned to sing in

the Yiddish language and style fairly convincingly. She has even specialized in the songs of Mordecai Gebirtig, the martyred Krakow Yiddish
poet-songwriter whose work has been revived in Italy and Germany.
Ladislaw, Irina's performing partner, has adopted Jewish stylistic features
on his clarinet and electric piano, and he appears onstage wearing a *yarmulke*, the Jewish skullcap. They explain their attachment to Jewish performance through their origins in Przemysl, a Polish-Jewish town of pre-
war fame where, they say, they absorbed the sounds of Jewish music.

Itzhak Perlman. A year or two before this week in October, a film crew
captured Itzhak Perlman and his all-star klezmer backup bands as they
traveled to Kazimierz. Perlman had only recently entered the klezmer scene
from his permanent perch atop the classical virtuoso world. In the resulting film, *In the Fiddler's House*, the violinist makes some pointed legit-
imizing moves. The first narrative scene of the film shows Perlman looking in from outside the gates of a Renaissance Jewish synagogue. He tells
us that Poland is where the music started. Inside, representing the dead
Yiddish culture of the city, the American klezmer band Brave Old World,
with violinist Deborah Strauss, is playing a very non-Polish-origin style of
Jewish music, the Rumanian *doina*, the signature piece of the modern
klezmer movement's quest for authenticity. Strauss has learned klezmer
style mostly from Kurt Bjorling, the brilliant clarinetist-cymbalist of
Brave Old World. This scene represents multiple ironies and chronotopic
overlays and I will leave it to the reader to analyze them.

Kazimierz was the backdrop for imaginary Jewish community even earlier, at the time noted Polish director Jerzy Kawalerowicz filmed *Austeria*
(1983) using one of the buildings on the square as a set. *Austeria* tells the
story of a group of Jews on the first day of World War I in 1914, hiding in
a Jewish-run inn from marauding Cossack troops. Music plays a key role
in the director's vision of Jewish community as he focuses primarily on a
cluster of Hasidim surrounding their *tzadik* (spiritual leader). For long
stretches, they break into ecstatic prayer-songs, most pointedly at the end
of the film, when the Hasidim, singing and dancing, throw off their clothes
and jump into the pond naked, only to be blasted by artillery fire, presumably a previsioning of the Holocaust. Throughout, these ultra-Ortho-
dox Jews, set off from the world, speak in Polish, the language of the ac-
tors. It is just one more of those typical ironies of modern Polish-Jewish
representation and brings the 1983 *Austeria* in line with today's Kazimierz
entertainments.

Just as the plight of Kawalerowicz's fictional community (based on a
story by the Polish-Jewish writer Julian Strykowski) acts as precursor to
the Holocaust, it also resonates as a cinematic forerunner to the English-
speaking Krakow community invented by Steven Spielberg for *Schindler's
List*, filmed in the same neighborhood, for which the great Hollywood film

composer John Williams invented a musical chronotope of his own. Like the inventive performers of Kazimierz, Williams found he could convert traditional Yiddish tunes into a symbol of past community, relying mainly on the beloved song "Oyfn pripetshok." It is sung in the film by an Israeli children's choir at one of the visual and emotional high points—the liquidation of the Krakow ghetto. Here Williams falls into line with Spielberg's teleological vision of the Holocaust as being redeemed in the creation of the State of Israel. The klezmer reference of the film score comes in the person of Itzhak Perlman, who, we have already seen, has made a point of personally identifying with Krakow. So do the thousands of Israeli schoolchildren who act as living embodiments of Spielberg's vision by coming to Kazimierz (and nearby Auschwitz) to look for the ghosts of the Jewish past.

These chimeric communities of artistic imagination have superseded any real presence; the perhaps 150 Jews of contemporary Krakow hardly act as a counterweight to the fictitious Jewish settlements just described. It is the competing cafes of Kazimierz's main square that do that job today, and the wildly arbitrary music helps even more than the stock *gefilte fish* of the menu to tantalize the visitor with the idea of a missing community. Kazimierz deserves full-scale analysis and has already received some scholarly attention as a place of pilgrimage, but as a site for music-making, less has been said. The term "phantom community" here might help to signal overlapping chronotopes: (1) the imaginary time that visitors fuse with the space, and (2) the presumed authenticity of the music that melds a number of fantasies shared by audiences with a wide variety of musicians in the common space-time of heritage presentations. The term "entertainment" actually suits the situation better than "presentation" but seems as odd a word as one might find to describe how people pass their "time" in a haunted square centered on a disappeared population.

True to the fate of Eastern European Jewry, the place to find "real" Krakow Jewish music is Melbourne, Australia, where Leo Rosner, who grew up with the tradition, has been a fixture as an ethnic entertainer for over fifty years since emigrating there in 1949. Rosner, who was one of the Jews saved by Oscar Schindler, grew up in a klezmer family, which meant he studied classical violin and played tangos and foxtrots in the local nightclubs (Netsky 1998). To create authentic Krakow klezmer music, then, would not mean to sing Gebirtig songs as a core Jewish repertoire, but, along with a few Jewish wedding favorites, to play the dance music of the 1930s, much of which was written by Jewish pop songwriters.

But even the existence of a Jewish space without Jews does not automatically imply the Krakow solution, as Judith Cohen's work in Ribadavia, Spain, tells us. There, in an isolated town of 3,000 with only two recently arrived Jewish families, heritage events commemorating the large medieval Sephardic Jewish community take place annually. Since 1993 the local Spaniards have presented a Sephardic mock wedding with such enthusiasm that a group of local women now confidently feel themselves to be "authentic" in performance and have even convinced Spanish Jews in Madrid that Ribadavia "must" be a Jewish town that has preserved medieval Jewish folklore (Cohen 1997). Perhaps it is the 500-year absence of Jews from the town that allows this degree of cultural play, whereas in Krakow, Polish memories of the Jews and their recent fate seems to rule out any local crossover urges beyond dancing in the streets when American klezmer bands come to town. We are certainly not likely to see groups of Krakowians staging a Jewish wedding in the Kazimierz square anytime soon.

Europe also boasts of an ever-expanding number of developing klezmer cities. Along with the already mentioned phantom sites, there are also some phoenix klezmer communities in Russia and Ukraine, places like Kishinev, Chernovits, Vinnitsa, and Odessa that actually once rang to the sound of klezmorim, where Jews, and sometimes non-Jews, are bringing back that tradition. In some cases, Western aid is helping to revive vanished communal feelings through musical intervention, even in so large a site as St. Petersburg, where an annual American-sponsored "Klezfest" began in 1998. Ironically, unlike the cities just mentioned, St. Petersburg was hardly a klezmer capital in the past, since its small Jewish community existed under the fiercely restrictive residential rule of the Russian Empire and was nearly annihilated during the siege and evacuation of the city during World War II.

For the current large population of Petersburg Jews (over 100,000), klezmer is slowly becoming one choice in the whole array of possible ways to identify with Jewish culture. Not quite a phoenix situation, Petersburg might become a klezmer community of reaffiliation for those connecting with some past notion of Jewishness in ways not dissimilar from Kurland's Massachusetts situation, where secularized, assimilated Jews are turning to their roots. Of course, surface similarities belie the deep differences of the American and post-Soviet situations. But perhaps we are seeing the convergence of lifestyles across the transatlantic space as the deep divisions of the twentieth century recede in memory.

Finally, Europe offers the opposite phenomenon, the coincidental klezmer community built by emerging bands who bring music to audiences unaffected by the histories of the affiliation communities described above. Of course, nothing is completely coincidental, as I tried to indicate in discussing motivation. Yet this music system demands that we think through the operation of the completely contingent, the accidental and the immediate. I have already mentioned one such moment, when the Bologna band Dire-Gelt plays in southern Italy and older women dressed in black get up and dance the tarantella to a Yiddish *freylekhs*. This is happening in a country not only where was there never a klezmer tradition, but where today there is no Jewish population to support it. The kind of community a band might create through the overlap of local traditions with the residue of *yiddishkayt* Italian style seems a wonderful coincidence, a special chronotope of the moment that is even beyond the term "phantom."

Also in Italy, the shows put on by Moni Ovadia are showcases of coincidence. He tells his rapt, overflow audiences that he, a Sephardic Jew from Bulgaria, came to the East European tradition by chance, in a Hasidic *shtibl* (study group) in Milan. The makeup of his band continues the theme of coincidence, including a pickup group of a Hungarian violinist masquerading as a Transylvanian folk fiddler, a genuine Russian baian (button accordion) player, and two Italians on clarinet and guitar. He structures his evenings through pure feeling, mixing emotional recitation of Yiddish verse with heartfelt renditions of cantorial items and what he calls klezmer, a mishmash of motifs.

It was at a 1997 Ovadia concert in Bologna that I had a moment of epiphany about klezmer's voyage into uncharted cultural waters. Dozens of prospective listeners had been turned away by police at the entrance to the Great Hall of the ancient University of Bologna, as unlikely a place for klezmer as one can imagine. As the Russian baianist played a Soviet mock-folk theme and variations, a cloud of Stalinism descended on the stage. I had a vision of *yiddishkayt*, that one-word wrapup of the folkways of Eastern European Jews, awaking from its dormancy and discovering it was still in a nightmare—its past and essence could be shaped at will by strangers. As Ovadia went into his recitation of the Hebrew prayer for the dead, "El mole rakhamim," my vision turned to anger. The last time I had heard this prayer was three months back at my father's funeral. Now Ovadia was chanting it on stage and, in the middle, realizing he had forgotten something, was fumbling into his pocket to find the *yarmulke*, the required hat for prayers, and to slap it onto his head. The overflow crowd took this all in breathlessly. My conclusion was this: the klezmer tradition, indeed all of *yiddishkayt*, is defenseless. The arbitrariness of Ovadia's work spills over to his audience, who note down the bits of information and misinformation he scatters through the evening. At one point he prefaced a klezmer piece with the "fact" that it was by that great master Naftule Rosenblatt, apparently conflating the legendary clarinetist Naftule Brandwein with the equally legendary cantor Yosele Rosenblatt. There is no local Jewish population or international klezmer nerve center that can react to these stimuli, which pass on to the adoring audience a set of contingent and coincidental impressions of a night's entertainment, a tourist excursion to a vanished culture. After the concert I asked Ovadia whether he might extend his work to a treatment of his own Sephardic tradition. He seemed genuinely surprised by the question and answered, "No, it would be too close to me."

Far from these crowds, in the Austrian Alps, to what community is the band Gebrider Moischele appealing as a group of Tyrolese folkie musicians dabbling in Yiddish culture? Here is their artistic credo: "We want to make music that touches. Music that inspires us to laugh, dream, and cry. Music that grew out of the feelings, longings, and dreams of ordinary people. Simply jiddish [sic] folk music!" (Gebrider Moischele 1995). Here the coincidental reaches out to the universal for support, invoking an accidental community of CD buyers that will become bonded by recognition of deeply held, common human values uniting in a utopian chronotope of feeling.

This move toward a noncontextualized structure of feeling is common in European liner notes and concert programs. One of the bands that calls itself *goyim* (non-Jews, gentiles) is Gojim of Vienna. They have been working for ten years at infiltrating Austrian entertainment with Jewish materials, outsiders recognizing what it takes to draw other outsiders into an ethnic-based feeling of community through universalizing the music's appeal. For their first album, a 1987 effort presenting Jewish workers' songs, they managed to get Austrian Communist Party funding on the basis of the general themes involved, at a moment when Austria was beginning to acknowledge its ambiguous role in the adoption and carrying out of Nazism. From this start they have repeatedly tried to find ways of moving in-group materials out of context and into local sensibilities. Their 1998 album takes a collection of poems written by Yiddish writers in Vienna before World War II and sets them in a wide variety of contemporary and anachronistic musical styles, ranging from Kurt Weill through rock and roll. This mix stresses their "goyish" angle of vision on Jewish materials and provides bridges from the poems to a coincidental community they are trying to build around their performances. Even more contingent is Gojim's tour of the Baltic states. Financed by Austrian government funding, this non-Jewish Viennese band went to Lithuania, Latvia, and Estonia, all former Soviet republics with a long history of suppression of Jewish culture, and played Jewish-based music for local audiences of Jews and non-Jews. Quite a few accidents of history had to occur for this very temporary community of players and listeners to form around traces of klezmer. Many such outreach efforts seem arbitrary, such as Leon Pollak's invitation to perform for a Kafka conference in Bari, Italy, offering the opposite example of a Jewish musician playing for a non-Jewish event.

Pollak, who plays mostly for non-Jews, stands at the intersection of various communities. Earlier I cited him in connection with the notion of multiculturalism; here I will place him a bit more in the Austrian context and let him speak for himself about his philosophy of klezmer. Pollak is quite aware of the coincidental nature of his audience, and also of his own pathway to Jewish music performance. He comes from Poland and went to Vienna from Israel. Accidentally discovering the possibility of marketing his own band, Ensemble Klesmer, he has navigated the contingencies of history warily but happily, enjoying the opportunity for expression of his own artistry and of his heritage. Unpacking just one sentence from his interview delineates the complexity here. Speaking about how you need to have a whole range of Jewish music in your ear to do things right, he says, "You have to have felt, and experience, and heard a lot, just the way I learned *wienermusik* [traditional Viennese popular music] here." The first half of the sentence speaks to rootedness, the second to contingency. In fact, Pollak's ensemble includes just two other musicians: one is a Bulgarian immigrant who can play all the Balkan/Central European styles, and the other is a native Viennese bass player, the one who exposed Pollak to *wienermusik*. Thus the band itself forms a coincidental community that can appropriately form the links between the music and the accidental audience.

Also in Austria, we move to Graz, where an American named Peter Harow, who changed his name to Joshua Horowitz, has established a base for serious klezmer research and has organized a succession of bands that insist on authenticity, playing (very effectively) in a style that he feels reconstructs the klezmer sound of 1900. He and Leon Pollak used to play together but parted over aesthetic issues, such as how much vibrato can be allowed in klezmer violin performance. For an American to insist on "authenticity" while an East European Jew can adapt to *wienermusik* foregrounds the arbitrariness of how klezmer chips fall: as they may.

Under the sign of contingency, authenticity becomes even more vexed an issue than in the course of a slowly evolving roots system. The question is: who is the judge, the arbiter of taste, for a coincidental audience? Pollak is very aware of the many branches on which he could become entangled, insisting on his right to personal interpretation even as he maintains a stance of continuity as someone who grew up with the tradition. Pollak's sensibility thrives on the deep emotions he feels in the music, and clearly he hopes that electric charge will galvanize the audience as well:

Each music reflects what the people and its culture make out of everyday life . . . a very particular music arose from these conditions. My attitude is that it's a completely emotion-tied, passionate music. Yearning, yearning for Jerusalem, for release, this supplication— these are not scholarly explanations. We feel history the same way today: we know that we're happy/lucky [*glücklich*], it's a relatively happy/lucky time living here in this democracy, but we never forget what happened here 50, 60 years ago . . . we carry this as Jewish human beings, just like the blacks in America or Africa.

[MS. What do your non-Jewish listeners hear?] I think they discover a lot for themselves, the coming back to the most simple, most basic, a little emotional, which comes from the heart. People feel immediately whether it's convincing, comes from the heart, or whether it's just imitation, only fast notes. If it's spoken from the heart and well played, then it speaks to them, that's communication. . . . Maybe the artist has to be more sensitive and transmit that to other people; that's what they come to the concert hall for. They want to experience something.

A final Austrian representative of klezmer is Isaac Loberan. A bass and accordion player of classical and Soviet popular music, Loberan happened to arrive in Vienna from Kishinev (now the capital of Moldova) on tour in 1991 and stayed as an asylum seeker. Now he returns to the Bukovina-Moldova-Odessa zone of klezmer origins not only to pick up musical inspiration, but to perform for the local Jewish communities, again with Austrian government funding. Returning the "Austrian" culture of klezmer to the former Austro-Hungarian lands where that music flourished offers yet another example of klezmer contingency. While some chronotope or other is in play here, and some putative appeal to "community" is invoked and sometimes realized, we will have to forge ahead into more challenging theoretical directions to assimilate this sort of musical interactivity.

The looseness of the linkages described here perhaps explains why, for many European contexts, the word "klezmer" is applied extremely loosely, or not at all: unlike the countless American combo-names with the prefix "klez-" (Klezmatics, Klezmeydlakh . . .), it is rarely part of a band name in Europe except in unusual cases like Leon Pollak's Ensemble Klesmer. A frequent move in naming a band is to co-opt a Yiddish or Hebrew phrase— *Kol Simcha, Zol zayn freylekh*—or an entirely imaginary Jewish-sounding word like one that a young Berlin band coined, La'om. At once dedicated to and somewhat distanced from klezmer, members of La'om are tickled that people stumble over and try to interpret their band name.

European klezmer will continue to keep a fairly tangential tie to community life beyond the need for cultural tourism in places like Prague and Krakow or the demand for local culture in phoenix cities like Budapest, Vienna, and potentially Warsaw. The most recent heritage project there is the reconstruction of a half-block of Jewish tenement houses on ulica Prosna that managed to survive the wartime annihilation of the Warsaw Ghetto by being located a few meters away from the wall. Doubtless, new strains of "klezmer" will echo off the restored walls of the rebuilt street. We will probably see a klezmer guidebook in the near future in an attempt to rationalize the very sporadic, contingent appearance of that musical system in European life.

I have brought up these sometimes problematic, sometimes coincidental European klezmer communities partly as a foil to the more coherent American nuclei of klezmer action, although a certain random motion of the molecules is evident on the western edge of the Atlantic as well. One way that klezmer communities will stabilize in the transatlantic grid will be through electronic linkages, flashes of energy across the cultural synapses that are slowly providing an ever-more reliable transmission pattern and network of relationships. Already, touring information is routinely distributed and websites are proliferating. Yet ultimately the sense of space and implied time—the catalogue of chronotopes—created by klezmer-related modes of performance remains intensely local. Musicians and audience alike are caught in a net of notes, words, sighs, and the familiarity of expected genres. We have only just begun to switch our sensors to the force field around that chronotopal experience, the core of attraction that informs any search for the klezmer community.

That experience is grounded in energizing performances, so we turn next to a consideration of music in action. I will attempt not an overall analysis, but rather a selective study of just some of the many channels and codes—the colors and flavors—that klezmer pieces offer players and audiences.

5

Klezmer Style as Statement

M any are the methods for "analyzing" music, as if it were a chemical component of consciousness, a substance that can be assayed, weighed, and measured for its intrinsic qualities. Among heritage musics, the klezmer repertoire does not submit easily to this sort of scrutiny. Suppose you were a researcher at the Hungarian Academy of Sciences. Your starting point would be hundreds of thousands of recorded and notated examples of peasant folk songs. In fireproof closets you would have securely stowed the almost sacred tune transcriptions, dating back to the dawn of the twentieth century, penned by the legendary composer-analysts Béla Bartók and Zoltán Kodály. Or suppose you were in Bucharest, where I once (1974) met a team of returning ethnomusicologists who were following up the "Bartók singers" yet again, to track the evolution of the folk aesthetic over three generations. "Oh," one said pointing to a newly transcribed melody, "Maria ends that line differently."

We have no such resources for klezmer. Long ago, tyrants and madmen destroyed or silenced the vast majority of the players. Across the huge expanse of the old klezmer territory, no one—save one heroic scholar in Kiev, Moshe Beregovski—organized extensive fieldwork or compiled a substantial archive of the tunes. In the United States—not surprisingly, given the ideology of assimilation—no counterpart to Beregovski emerged beyond the record producers of the commercial companies, who left us a legacy of 78 RPM recordings ignored by the academic world for decades. Only in the last few years has anyone thought to question retired musicians about the dried-up manuscripts in their attics. Until 1994 no one published a single serious, well-researched article in English on the nature and evolution of the core klezmer repertoire, so Walter Zev Feldman's essay stands like a solitary oak in a field of scholarly silence.

This chapter cannot compensate for so much destruction and neglect. All I plan to do is to extend the points made in earlier chapters in the direction of musical practice. One of ethnomusicology's basic tenets is that existing musical performance embodies general principles of group memory, personal artistry, and collective understanding. I will limit myself to methods and examples that I hope support those principles. To do so, I will call upon two familiar approaches: the "biography" of a tune—snapshots from its long life—and players' commentaries on performance, to illuminate three questions: How do modern players understand the older repertoire that has now become a modern canon? How do they conceptualize their technique? How do they arrive at personal style?

About the repertoire as a whole, one of the few comprehensive overviews comes from Feldman, who identifies four layers: (1) the "core repertoire," which "contains the most Jewish body of klezmer music and principally features the freylekhs (literally "happy"), a line dance performed to various melodies characterized by their lively interchange with Jewish religious music" as well as other genres of celebration like the sher; (2) the "transitional or southern repertoire, which consists mostly of dance tunes with Romanian-derived names" like bulgarish, honga, sirba, hora, doina; (3) "the co-territorial repertoire," which "consisted of local non-Jewish dances played by klezmorim for non-Jews, as well as for Jews within a limited geographical region," such as the Polish mazurka, Ruthenian kolomeyka, and Ukrainian kozachok"; (4) "the cosmopolitan repertoire" of items from Western Europe, like the quadrille, polka, and waltz (Feldman 1997). While this is only a provisional classification, it offers a usable road map of the klezmer repertoire. There is a strong underlying assumption: audience response drives what klezmer bands play, just as true today as it was a hundred years ago. Before we look at specific to cases, here is a capsule statement about musical materials, in the form of a rundown of interlocking conceptual components and a roundup of technical parameters.

Musical Resources

Aesthetic: a set of predispositions. "You can't go wrong if you leave something out," a remark made by the violinist Deborah Strauss to a student, reveals an aesthetic of restraint. It emerged in the same 1997 teaching session as "There's a tremendous beauty in being able to hold back." Another musician would be unlikely to make this sort of statement, preferring grittiness and sensuality of tone, or even encouraging the student to consider letting loose. Individual players all rely on the same set of early recordings as source material, and most agree on certain limits to collective taste, yet they follow different artistic roads, according to taste and temperament.

While this is true for many heritage systems, for klezmer these issues predominate in the absence of an unbroken line of performance practice. Always an individualized tradition, klezmer's contemporary condition favors the personal aesthetic over the collective consensus.

The search for an overall klezmer aesthetic has not yet begun. A place to start might be this remark from veteran Max Epstein: "Never play it twice the same way—never" (1999 interview with Hankus Netsky), or it may be the generally acknowledged sense that instruments, to be successful aesthetically, need to sound like voices, an orientation that can be found as far back as nineteenth-century Yiddish fiction.

Affect: as used here, a combination of the old English meaning of "mental disposition" (*Oxford English Dictionary*) and the music theory term *affekt* or "affection," the mood of a performed piece that arouses a similar mood in the listener. In the Jewish case, the spiritual connotations of songs that have become instrumental tunes can breathe a particular atmosphere into the music. More mundanely, the aesthetic choices made by modern bands mean that each piece on an album might have its own affect, or we can sense an individual or band affect—perhaps an attitude—that informs a body of work, the way Alicia Svigals describes the Klezmatics' "background hum," where they think they're "coming from." Affect might be thought of as an underlying assumption, a "take" on the piece's nature and its emotional weight. The choice of affect is like the breath you take before you lift the bow.

Affect might also describe the preconceptions audiences bring with them to klezmer concerts or that critics impute to the music. For example, if you had attended a concert by Leon Pollak's Viennese band Ensemble Klesmer in Prague in 1994, your hearing would have been tuned by remarks in the program notes by one Peter Pokorny, whose nutshell description of the affective charge of klezmer music specifies "an emotional character balanced between sensitive brilliance and euphoric dance fervour, an ironic view and also a passionate attempt to create a cantabile style."

Function: the social resonance of performance, including the contemplative nature of concert music, the animation of dance music, or the private pleasures of album-based listening. Klezmer contexts have been expanding for decades, moving out from the strictly live, celebratory sphere to the sit-down concerts and integrated albums of recent decades. At this point we can tick off a list of presumed "functions," but we don't know much about ways klezmer consumers integrate the music into their daily lives.

Style: a set of technical-aesthetic features and gestures that create a musical profile, allowing listeners instantly to identify—perhaps to pigeonhole—a type of music, a band, or a performer. Style components are easy to teach, especially now that klezmer has centralized transmission points (workshops, institutes) as well as an ever-increasing body of recorded work to emulate and to use as springbboards for personal stylistic moves. So Max Epstein, talking about how to play a Yiddish theater song, says, "You accent your high notes and slur down—expression!" (1999 interview with Hankus Netsky), he is describing a particular stylistic move attached to a specific genre. Style is the raw material for affect and is shaped by an aesthetic the way hand tools are designed to perform specific tasks.

Genre: a named, known type of piece (sher, freylekhs, doina. . .). Genres arise from an equation involving affect + style + function + memory of prior performance. Certain genres have become dominant in the klezmer world and are expected of any self-respecting band. An ability to play a passable doina shows you've reached a point of seriously understanding reflective, possibly improvisatory, stylistic and affective resources. Knowing enough dance tunes of the sher, bulgar, and freylekh core repertoire to enliven a wedding or concert is essential and can be judged by crowd response.

Item: a specific example of a genre or of a performer's personal repertoire, a named "tune" or "song." The recorded canon is restricted, offering a limited number of items, so players dig around in published or manuscript sources for fresh items to add to the list, not an easy task for this micromusic. The standard items have a larger-than-life importance in players' and audience's minds, since the same few pieces tend to be heard or to be worked on over and over, like the "Russian sher" or "Der heyser bulgar" among dance tunes, or the Solinski violin fantasies among listening pieces.

Medium: the preferred technological choice of a musician, usually a given instrument, with its own set of expectations about style and affect. Klezmer is unusually limited in this regard, since the clarinet sound of the 78 RPM era is so dominant, especially as recorded by Dave Tarras and Naftule Brandwein. The violin, once essential to the klezmer sound, was much less recorded, so its use today requires a very active effort of reconstruction that will be detailed later. The flute, extremely common in Eastern Europe, has yet to make a breakthrough into modern klezmer consciousness. The *tsimbl,* or cymbalom, the hammered dulcimer of Central and Eastern Europe, was reintroduced by Walter Zev Feldman (on his 1979 album with Andy Statman) and has become a less rare instrument, largely thanks to the work of Kurt Bjorling, Joshua Horwitz, and Stuart Brotman.

Model: individuals to emulate, through diligently studying their technical mastery and their originality. I've just mentioned the Tarras–Brandwein influence, but lesser-known figures can impress certain players in strong ways. Max Weissman, for example, made one extraordinary recording of the "Gas-nign," a much-recorded core item, then he disappeared from history. We know nothing of the man beyond that single side, the result of three minutes before a microphone one day in 1920. In the music culture of scarcity that is klezmer, his take on that favored piece can be an important fact. For violinists, Joseph Solinski is a crucial ancestor; his few recorded pieces are technically demanding and aesthetically advanced, and they were actually produced in Europe, where only about 10 percent of the available recorded repertoire originated. Yet we know no more about him than we do Max Weissman. Alicia Svigals likes to tell the story of accidentally finding a Joseph Solinski in the Manhattan phone book and rushing to call him on the off chance that the legendary fiddler was yet alive ("sorry, wrong number . . ."). Our inability to place such key masters generationally or geographically is really frustrating and makes the relationship of a modern performer to "the tradition" a very vexed issue.

Items live only when they are played, and it is hard to know exactly which aspects of performance to focus on for analysis. Music is multichanneled to begin with, and as a tune ages, it picks up more and more layers of codes and registers of expression. As Ciaran Carson puts it eloquently about Irish music, "Each tune has a catalogue of variations within the time, and genealogies of memory, so that the huge ornate system can be entered anywhere, for any point will lead you to a destination or a halt en route that might prove more interesting than what you thought you might be looking for" (Carson 1996:89). There has been almost no work done on the performance practice of the klezmer repertoire. Unwilling to be encyclopedic, here is a selective outline of some of the factors that strike the ear while one is listening attentively to a rendition of a klezmer tune.

Listening Resources

Form. The repertoire includes items in a variety of shapes, some more restricted than others. Rather than the more rhapsodic, "listening" repertoire, I will discuss the sectional, up-tempo tunes. Feldman is right to call this the "core repertoire," since an ability to play sequences of danceable, foot-tapping melodies has always put bread on the klezmer's table.

Tunes usually have two or three sections, repeated over and over in a cycle until, intuitively, it's time to move on to the next item in the string of melodies. Each section is a cluster of subsections, small units of form that can often be subdivided into even tinier, but very active, cells. Beginnings are usually distinctive, as are cadences, the phrase or section endings that

Example 5.1. Classic klezmer cadence.

signal closure. Virtually all historic, and most contemporary, performances of these tunes end with the same keynote-affirming, formulaic cadence, the thumbprint of klezmer music (ex. 5.1).

In performance, tunes are linked to build shorter or longer suites, sets
of melodies that may be customarily or personally connected. The logic of
this process was badly interrupted by the advent of the three-minute 78
RPM recording, which isolated tunes from each other, and newer CD albums do not tend to offer explanations for sequencing, though the more
articulate bands often imply an integrated aesthetic at the level of overall
album presentation. Max Epstein is critical of modern bands' lack of interest in sequencing: "Don't follow with the same thing," he advises (interview with Netsky, 1999).

Tonality. There is no published work that details the complexities of
tonal organization in the klezmer repertoire. Sections and even subsections often shift their tonal orientation. It is easy to notice some tenden-
cies, but the implicit logic of klezmer tonal thinking is fluid and elusive.
We await a full-scale study of tonality as a cultural concept among Eastern European Jews. What we have repeatedly gotten are arbitrary at-
tempts to bundle the available examples under blankets called "modes" or
the like, shortchanging the flexibility and ambiguity of traditional practice
in vocal and instrumental styles.

Intonation. No one plays klezmer strictly "in tune" from the point of
view of the classically accepted, equal-tempered scale on the piano, as the
reader will notice while listening to the CDs accompanying this book. In
all musics, clarinetists and violinists have great latitude to bend and shape
pitch, and the klezmer repertoire is no exception. Feldman (interview,
1998) reports playing Alicia Svigals's 1997 album *Fidl* for a group of knowledgeable Turkish musicians in Istanbul, a milieu famous for its great sensitivity to fluctuations and systematizations of pitch organization. After
listening intently, they reported that they found the music quite system-
atic from a modal point of view. However, Svigals herself disavows any
"system," saying she plays intuitively. Given the small sample of performers and recordings we have, with their random generational and spatial
spread, it would be extremely difficult to establish any standard definition
of intonational thinking in the klezmer world of yore. Today there is still
no discourse on this topic among musicians, and they do not (in my experience) feature it much in their teaching. I introduce this topic not to

offer a solution, but to demonstrate the tentative and tenuous nature of our understanding of klezmer theory and method.

Many issues arising from listening to klezmer can be found as easily in . other folk-origin styles. Here is another telling passage from Ciaran Carson on Irish music, this time about how to find the pitch for a tune: "The song is always open to negotiation . . . how you do depends on the circumstances: on the state of your lungs and vocal cords and diaphragm and larynx; on the state of the room or the stage or the hotel foyer; on the state of the audience; on the state of your brain; on what went before and what might come after; on what you've eaten or drunk or smoked; on the relative humidity and temperature" (Carson 1996:163).

Ornamentation. For all the reticence around the performance of klezmer music, this parameter stands out as the one that has generated the most pervasive discourse. Susan Bauer (1996), a German researcher investigating New York klezmer, was surprised to notice just how much discussion there was in this area of practice. Some reasons come to mind for the almost obsessive interest in the little twists and turns, sighs and trills, of klezmer performance. In the cluster of European and American musics that surround klezmer, the typical ornamentation patterns of Jewish performers have always been one of the most distinctive features of the style. There are parallels in other spheres. Observers often commented on the related sound of cantors in the "golden age" of the cantorate (first half of the twentieth century, roughly). Since one of the axioms of the klezmer world has long been that instrumental style is most successful when it emulates vocal style, perhaps the linkage holds even today among sensitive players who have not been overly influenced by an instrumental aesthetic of sheer virtuosity or technical excellence.

In America, commentators felt that the Jewish vocal aesthetic was underlay the "tear in the voice" that made singers like Al Jolson and songwriters like Irving Berlin stand out in popular music history. The subtle, supplicative style favored by Eastern European Jews was even remarked on by Feldman's Istanbul listeners, who thought Svigals's playing was suffused with the "laughter through tears" sound so often associated with Jewish music. Even the great Russian composer Dmitri Shostakovich endorsed this characterization. Given the prevalence of such an attitude about affect, it makes sense to privilege ornamentation as the place to look for "Jewishness." Whether the word "ornament" itself is a help or a hindrance to an understanding of musical practice is a subject I will return to soon.

Diving into the discourse around ornament brings one to submerged layers of aesthetic about the nature of melody that are surprisingly deep, among both the older generation of klezmorim and their modern successors. Max Epstein, a giant of an old-timer who has become a walking textbook for younger musicians, says: "It's the melody—you've got everything there—and you're filling in the empty spots," implying there are structural spaces that demand an appropriate emotional-technical rounding out with a small gesture in the right place: "It's got to be a part of you that you're expressing," but also "It's gotta match, it's gotta fit into its place. . . . The whole thing about music is, if you're going to embellish it—the right place. You've got to know the right place, and you can't teach that" (interview with Netsky, 1999). Despite Epstein's warning, younger klezmer masters do teach "ornamentation" all the time, at formal sessions in workshop contexts or, as in the case of Andy Statman, on an instructional video. Echoing Epstein's concerns, Statman says philosophically: "Ornaments are a way of bringing out the heart that's inside the melody." A few minutes later he turns to the technical: "Although you can use it freely, it's very specific. If it's used incorrectly, you can tell someone doesn't really understand the style." Statman also cites Dave Tarras on the evils of overornamentation, which "damages the spirituality of the melodies" (Statman 1997). This fine-tuned combination of expressive individuality, group spirituality, and conventional expertise reveals just how difficult it is to pick apart "style," to separate the technical from the cultural.

Tone color. It is not ornamentation alone that generates this "Jewish sound." Tone color, another hard-to-discuss musical parameter, is inseparable from notions of melodic-ornamental expression, but it tends to be less discussed, except about given instruments—notably the clarinet and violin—and certain masters, most famously Tarras and Brandwein. But many shadings of timbre and ornament can be found in the stylings of the older klezmer instruments. For example, the way the wire strings of the tsimbl were pounded or stroked helped specify an identifiable "Jewish" sound in the multiethnic East European musicians' milieu.

Affect. This factor was discussed earlier, so I will just restate it here as a precondition for listening. Players decide on an affect—up-tempo dance tune, meditative melody—and stick with it throughout the piece. A slow-to-fast suite is also a statement of affect, suggesting a standardized shift of moods. While in the older recordings, affects might be fairly stable across performers for the same items, today's klezmorim can be quite arbitrary in their decisions, as we'll see in the case of a tune that has slowed down noticeably from its original 1925 recording. Others might speed up. Several musicians have remarked to me on a tendency in the early days of neo-klezmer to show off competence, to play things briskly and technically, followed by a more recent period of rethinking and personalizing affect.

ALL THE PARAMETERS JUST MENTIONED, along with many others not discussed, are so intertwined in performance as to be inextricable. Ornaments appear as structural markers; tone color helps produce affect, and so on.

Also important to remember is that these components of klezmer have an unbalanced history. Scarcely described in historical sources for the centuries before recorded sound, the music suddenly falls under the spotlight around 1910, creating a period of "high klezmer" in turbulent times. In those best-lighted decades of the early twentieth century, the music was undergoing such rapid transformation as a result of mass migration and the impact of recording itself that we have a very skewed notion of how it sounded and functioned in its Eastern European setting, and an almost garish picture of its nature in the age of recording. When scrutinized after 1975, the portrait blurs even further because of the strong personalities of both the few surviving old masters and the younger reconstructive musicians. The newcomers had a fierce stake in "reviving" the canonical repertoire, but an equal determination to show they had something new to offer.

In such micromusical systems, the fate of the components listed above maximized the importance of specific items. These are the fixed, known, reproducible units that can help the musician display mastery of the tradition while serving as springboards for personal expression. It is a situation reminiscent of the jazz community, with its requirement that you have the canon down cold before you try to impress anyone with your dazzling originality. The tendency of sound recording to stockpile items, to put them on the shelf as brand-name goods, makes them prominent in contemporary heritage systems. No commentary on the modern evolution of traditional Irish music fails to mention the outsized influence of the violinist Michael Coleman's early commercial recordings on the evolution of that tradition. Even for a heritage system as large as American "old-time" music, it is just a handful of collectors and performers and their favorite songs and tunes that have become the canon, and recordings have done most of the job of fixing the expectations, sculpting the profile, and staking out the territory. Think of the total arbitrariness of Elizabeth Cotten's influence on guitar picking, which came about because she was a domestic worker for the Seeger family. And without the Seegers' boys—Pete and Mike—how would any narrative of "folk revival" have turned out?

To economize and to unify the analysis of klezmer style, I will focus on the violin, as played by the young women quoted in earlier chapters, and will concentrate on a handful of well-known pieces. As a violinist myself, I've been struck by the musicians' intense creativity in re-creating the sound of an instrument that has been so neglected in recent klezmer decades. The violin seems a perfect instrument for adaptive strategies, since so many people have domesticated it into such diverse traditions, ranging from Euro-North American folk musics through those as far removed as Burma and Colombia. As a recent country music song puts it, "If you're going to play in Texas, you better have a fiddle in the band."

The following short tune performance analyses will be limited to areas that show compositional logic, that is, the thinking that lies behind the way people put performances together. This mustering and clustering of resources in the service of coherent music-making should offer some insights into how klezmer operates today as a living, evolving musical tradition.

Case 1: "Dem Trisker Rebns Khosid"

The genre called the *khosidl* seems central to the core repertoire, since its very name, referencing the figure of the *khosidl*, or Hasid, evokes a deeply Jewish Eastern European milieu. The Hasidic movement, which began in the late eighteenth century, spread rapidly and broadly across that Jewish world, carrying with it certain attitudes about music that translate into a strongly charged affect in performance. Generalizing, we can say that Hasidim believed deeply in the spiritual power of the *nign* (from Hebrew *nigun*, a melody) to uplift believers, possibly even to move them toward a transcendental state of awareness of and union with God. Centered around a charismatic leader—the rebbe—who had a "court" in a chosen town, groups of Hasidim sang the nigunim of their leader's choice, which might be composed by a "court composer" or even by the rebbe himself. Many of these powerful melodies were sung without words, some for dancing. The tunes themselves, if not the contexts of performance, were shared by non-Hasidic Jews, as Beregovski points out in his unpublished 1940s collection of nigunim. Klezmorim played such melodies for the Hasidic circle, or simply absorbed them from the local soundscape into their non-Hasidic gigs. In its instrumental transformation, a nign might be called a khosidl, indicating its Hasidic origins. In this guise, the khosidl made its appearance at weddings and other klezmer performance events. For a fuller account of the khosidl, see Feldman 1994/2000 (Feldman has also generously shared his view of the genre's history with me in correspondence).

Dave Tarras recorded "Dem trisker rebns khosid" in September 1925, and it comes from the family repertoire of his southern Ukrainian homeland. The name he gave it refers to the rebbe of Trisk, presumably a Hasidic leader about whom he knew directly. He sang a vocal version for Feldman that was much slower than the recorded variant. I will compare Tarras's tune with three recent versions (mid 1990s) by the violinists Alicia Svigals and Deborah Strauss and the Flying Bulgar Klezmer Band.

This khosidl is in three sections. Though each section follows a different tonal route, they all end with the same cadence, a rather unusual structure. This means the sections line up at the ending, providing an overall

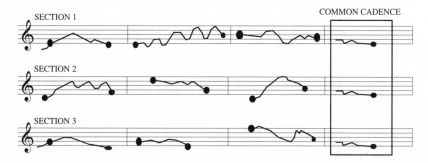

Example 5.2. "Trisker": contours of sections.

formal design as sketched out in example 5.2 (CD 1), which illustrates contour differences and similarities among the subsections of the three parts; the common line-ending cadence is boxed. Disregarding that cadence, sections 1 and 3 are more or less in minor, section 2 in major. The cadence and a couple of other moments play with alternate versions of pitches, most obviously the second scale degree, which can be either a half step or whole step away from the tonal center, here transcribed as E. The B above can be flat or natural (section 1), and another chromatic move (section 3) introduces a G-sharp that suggests the tune's interest in a minor-major alternation. The play with tonality is fairly modest in this tune; nigunim and klezmer melodies can offer much more complex sonic shifts. Klezmer tunes are like villagers: you can tell by the dialect and lifestyle that they all belong to the same locale, but each individual is easily recognizable and no two are alike.

Example 5.3 represents Tarras's performance in a fairly simple transcribed form. Tarras's clarinet style comes across in the details. Notice the slide halfway through section 1, from a note down (more or less a half step) then back up, bracketed with an X in the example. The effect is like the movement of a skateboarder from the edge of the ramp down, then back up to the opposite edge, or it might be visualized as a trampoline bounce that gives the player energy. This instrumental dip is just an amplification of a vocal mannerism of Eastern European Jewish folk singing, and Tarras uses it every time he plays the section. The second and third times around, he changes the opening gesture of section 1 by adding other slides that would not have been sung (see ex. 5.4). This gives the tune more variety at a highly recognizable spot—the beginning, with which the listener is already familiar. Is this slide "an ornament"? To my mind, that term is a worn-out generalization for a very large set of resources that canny klezmorim use for variation. The contrast between the bounciness of much of the playing with the sinuousness of the slides

Example 5.3. Tarras, "Dem trisker rebns khosid," 1925.

is a hallmark of classic klezmer clarinet style, perhaps even more fully worked out by Tarras's main rival, Naftule Brandwein.

One way to get at Tarras's compositional logic is to look more closely at the way he plays the same opening phrase differently in the four times he runs through the tune on the recording (ex. 5.4). The first time, he offers a tidy leap to E, followed by a crisp tour of the upper register of the tune, with a simple descent to E to close out the phrase. For the second appearance of section 1, Tarras decides to start quite high, snaking down through a double slide to the closing E. These slides mirror the slide to come, discussed above. The third time section 1 comes around, Tarras goes back to the original melodic motion, keeping the slides, but the fourth time, he makes a move reminiscent of the second variation, starting high and coming down through an arpeggio. Suddenly the arpeggio that opens phrase 2 has a partner that precedes it in opposite motion. This is an instrumentalist's way of thinking, a compositional logic different from the way someone would sing a contemplative nign.

Sharply etched, staccato delivery, combined with smooth slides, offer a platform for style, but there's another key component: the flicked-off

Example 5.4. Tarras's variations of the opening phrase of "Trisker."

pitches above and below the longer notes that impart energy to the line and emphasis to important tones. Four kinds of quick-note moves are characteristic of the core repertoire: (1) a fast note-higher reference, on the beat, before a longer note; (2) a brief departure-return, on the beat; (3) a trill, actually several types of trills, depending on the context; (4) the most "Jewish" of all, the *krekhts*, or *kneytsh*, which is notated in the example with a K, a quick move some distance upward after a note has been established that involves a special technique on any instrument, to be discussed "scientifically" later in this section.

In the first subsection of section 1, (ex. 5.3 again) Tarras is steady, thinking of the G in the G-F-E downward cadence as a place to stress through one of these "ornaments." The reason the word is in quotes is this: clearly, there's a strong tradition of using the emphasis of these minigestures for structural purposes, yet an "ornament" should be something superfluous. The same thing happens at the end of the section on the descending cadence F-E-D-E—the F gets a little turn that seems to mark the moment every time. Switching from one "ornament" to another in the same structural spot, then, becomes a way of offering the variety Tarras wants, to keep himself and the listener awake through the many repetitions of the sections. After all, in a wedding context he might play those sections, or ones with similar profiles, dozens of times before moving on. In fact, wedding musicians in many cultures playing many styles do just this sort of variation.

All these micromoves tend to be called "ornaments." We know that ornaments were important, because no less an authority on twentieth-century music than Arnold Schönberg said that "one could no more omit them than one could omit something similar in a construction of steel" (1978:344). Yet, as I signaled earlier, that term is less than informative about the way musicians sprinkle subtlety into their fluid, ongoing motion. We might think of ornaments in many different ways, perhaps as what the 1928 *Handbook of Irish Music* calls "the complicated graces so dear to music" (Carson 1996:96). What if we thought of the "ornaments" as diacritical marks? "Diacritical," says the *American Heritage Dictionary*, comes from the greek *"dia*, apart + *kronein*, to separate," and a diacritical mark is "added to a letter to indicate a special phonetic value." But in the Jewish tradition there's much more to this. A thousand years ago the sages invented a system of diacritical marks for the most sacred texts, the Pentateuch (first five books of the Hebrew Bible), the recitation of which is necessary for the unfolding of the Jews' weekly and yearly ritual cycle. They did this so that the scattered Jewish communities, who no longer spoke the language of the sacred text, would keep from turning it into inaccurate babble. It was of prime importance for cultural survival to keep the syntax and grammar of the chanted words clear and constant across the globe wherever Jews lived. Those marks, the *te'amim*, supply a musical— or at least prosodic—counterpart to the line of text. This is not to say that "ornaments" in klezmer have anything like the cultural charge of the *te'amim*, but we are dealing with a society that is centered on the performance and commentary of texts. In this way of thinking, a tune is a type of text: it too needs to stay familiar and accurate.

For the newcomer klezmorim of recent decades, the recordings of the older masters serve as texts. Instead of the strict scriptural model of the *te'amim*, the analogue to these texts might be the tradition of talmudic commentary, the idea that individually, locally, and generationally, the life of the ancient writings continues in a timeless way because their exegesis goes on and on over the centuries. The American klezmorim of the last two decades continually pay homage to the canon of their forefathers but feel free to make their own presence known in the tradition by adapting the principles of repetition, variation, and the ways of making melodic distinction. Here I might turn to the *Shorter Oxford English Dictionary* definition of "diacritic": "serving to distinguish; distinctive." The krekhts in particular serves not only to distinguish particular pitches structurally as part of the commentary on the tune, but more generally to mark Jewish music from the many surrounding krekhts-less styles, for while Romanians, Ukrainians, Greeks, and others have many gorgeous glides and turns, none sounds, or is used, quite like the klezmer krekhts.

"Diacritical" is just one way to interrogate the term "ornament." Most standard definitions prefer to place the word in another context, as part of a dialogue between "structure" and "ornament." The *New Oxford Companion to Music* issues the bald statment that "ornamentation is the decoration of a pre-existent melody line." I've seen a much livelier version of the structure–ornament relationship in a print ad for a luxury necklace in *The New Yorker:* "Only ornamentation can explain why the body gets thin at the neck and wide again at the shoulder," a witty reversal of the usual put-down of ornament as subordinate and superficial. There's a large literature on ornamentation in early classical music that takes up this issue, but the main author, Frederick Neumann (1978:3), has to concede on page 3 of his magnum opus that ornament and its complement, structure, "will usually combine in mixtures that defy clear separation."

Of course, ornament is more than a musical term; it is borrowed from the vocabulary of the visual arts. Michael Snodin and Maurice Howard, authors of a recent history of ornament in Europe since 1450, tell us that "ornament is both functional and contextual; it serves to relate one thing to another" (Snodin and Howard 1996:11). This ornament is very germane to the musical contexts of interest here. They also talk about "the notion, first expressed in ancient times, that there was a moral dimension to the use of ornaments" (ibid.: 12). By telling the tale of klezmer ornamentation, I am suggesting more broadly that we could use a more coherent comparative approach to a term I find both unchallenged and overburdened.

We now turn to the musicians themselves for commentary on their aesthetic approach, using two examples of how young violinists approach the Tarras "Trisker." Alicia Svigals's version (CD 2) arises from a long-term association with the Tarras original, since the piece was otherwise not recorded, but she says that when she turned to this tune, she had not heard the older version in a long time. When I played his version and hers back to back, she was surprised at how much slower her tempo was (quarter note = 77 instead of 92), and at some of the divergent aesthetic choices her recording reflects. These are rather modest, but worth a closer look. Her section 1 follows Tarras rather closely, and she plays it unchanged from repetition to repetition. It is in section 3 that she most strongly signals her individuality, prominently in the second time around (ex. 5.5). Going up to a higher register on the violin, she increases the number of krekhts sounds and bends the intonation more. This E-string

Example 5.5. Alicia Svigals, section 3 of "Trisker."

sound is a hallmark of Svigals's playing of the core repertoire; it combines with a distinctive timbre on the lower strings (that cannot be notated) to make a highly distinctive personal statement, a painstakingly developed trademark sound. Feldman has written a succinct summary of the instrument's earlier stylistic profile in klezmer (included in the liner notes for Svigals's album):

> The klezmer music [for fiddle] known to us has three principal sources: techniques shared with other forms of European folk fiddling, a tibre partly akin to Romanian Gypsy *lăutar* ("professional") fiddling, and a variety of ornaments and rhythmic phrasing coming from Jewish vocal sources. . . . Some of the recorded klezmer fiddlers had evidently absorbed techniques of classical Western violin playing as well, which must have become more widespread after Jews were permitted to attend conservatories in the Russian Empire during the last third of the nineteenth century. (Feldman 1997)

Svigals herself thoughtfully articulates her own aesthetic-technical position:

> [MS:how do you imagine the space of the violin as an arena where you work out your ideas?] I think I actually use the violin in an unviolinistic way in the sense that . . . I'm all over the place. I don't do things that are natural and easy—staying in first position, using open tuning, using fiddle stuff, old-timey; I want to do anything on the violin, so when I play, I've got the sound first and I make myself do whatever needs to be done physically to make the sound happen. And the sound that I've got is any melody that's out there and anything I can write that draws on that idiom, and played with this accent which I consider the klezmer fiddle accent, which is a repertoire of ornamentation and also a timbral thing, a certain kind of timbre that I get. Some of it is straight out of the old recordings, this krekhtsing, but some of it is, I use this timbre which is actually sort of stolen from Greek and Turkish fiddle playing. But I feel like if klezmer fiddlers weren't doing this before, they should have been. And so I'm correcting that gap in klezmer fiddle history, because to me it sounds so Jewish. It's like guttural kind of, it's got a lot of overtones in it. Maybe what I've got in my head is that it's folky, it's ethnic, it's got a rich envelope, it's not pure, it's not a metal flute, it's not a classically trained voice playing Schubert lieder, it's not a violin. It's got lots of overtones, it's very buzzy and guttural. So I try to get that timbre. I never thought about this because no one has asked me this before; it's got a kind of expressiveness—this is so hard to put into words—because it's really

a musical phenomenon—a kind of quality of expressiveness, quality in the sense of flavor, a really specific flavor that I think of as Jewish. When I say this, it sounds really stupid, because I don't believe in that kind of mystifying abstract stuff, because I really believe music is a concrete thing, but I try and get it with the ornamentation, with this timbral thing, which is a bow thing really, and that's what I'm doing. I'll do all kinds of uncomfortable violinistic things to get around the instrument. I can do it because I was classically trained; I'll do whatever needs to get done to play those melodies with this sound. It's really hard to describe. (Interview, 1996)

Asked about her special E-string sound, with its emphasis on the krekhts, she says:

What Zev [Feldman] calls the core repertoire, like the really Jewish stuff; the ornaments I tend to play are very much like cantorial singing, and they're like rubato singing. And there are other songs which are sort of pastoral sounding, often major key, things on the fiddle which have a very naive, pastoral sound. And I do another set of ornaments for those, like thin, high thin-wire E sounds with little sobs but no trills really, none of those vibrato trills, just a very taut, plain sound with lots of slides in between and sobs at the end. It wasn't deliberate, but now that you ask, I realize I differentiate those. Different tunes seem to call for those different sounds. (Interview, 1998)

Elsewhere, she remarks that in any case, you have to do something more pronounced on the E-string, since it's just a wire, whereas the lower, thicker violin strings offer more possibilities for the kind of timbral play she describes in the first quotation above.

Svigals's versatility makes her an ideal figure to help us understand current klezmer complexity. In her work with the internationally prominent band the Klezmatics, she has developed a style of almost dizzying intensity that relies on rock, jazz, and blues techniques. It is in this mode that she dazzles Itzhak Perlman in the film *In the Fiddler's House*. During a rehearsal with the Klezmatics, Perlman begs off playing solos as long as he can, and rolls his eyes when she plays. Svigals also composes pieces in core repertoire style. Her solo album of 1997, *Fidl*, from which the "Trisker" recording comes, is all related to that core, but she prefers not to feel it as "traditional," since she subtly introduces backup musicians here and there who reference non-Jewish, transnational traditional styles:

Everybody's—"Oh this is Alicia's trad album"—it's not trad, it's just from another contemporary sound. Instead of drawing on Led Zep-

pelin like we do in the Klezmatics, I draw on Joan Baez. It's a contemporary folky sound. Not so much my playing as the arrangement,
the production. It's psychedelic, when the rest of the band comes in,
the flute, it's that Celtic sound, Pentangle, Jethro Tull. Kind of reverby,
spacey—I think of that as contemporary. (Interview, 1998)

Deborah Strauss, another fine younger klezmer violinist, takes a very
different angle of approach to the "Trisker" piece. She recorded it around
the same time as Svigals, and I also videotaped her in 1997 teaching the
tune to a Wesleyan student, an undergraduate named Rachel Thompson,
who, as a total beginner, had an uncanny knack for picking up klezmer
fiddle style. Strauss's recorded performance is even slower than Svigals's,
taking the piece down from Tarras's 92/quarter note and Svigals's 77 to a
leisurely 64. Speaking of the Tarras original, Strauss says that "it really
moves along, and I turned it into something more laid back . . . an aesthetic of mine, but you should remember he learned it from a grandparent, who sang it, so you want to keep that as a basis." Here we have a
roots move that recognizes both Tarras's speeding up of a contemplative,
semi-sacred vocal version and a personal need by Strauss, a contemporary artist, to slow the tune back down. In effect, she is honoring not only
the "ancestor" Tarras, but his forefathers as well. Both Svigals and Strauss
credit the innate spiritual impetus of the tune that Tarras inherited with
inflecting their approach. This way of thinking might reflect the reaffir-
mation of klezmer's spirituality that has intensified in the late 1990s (Kirshenblatt-Gimblett 1998:54–56).

Strauss's way with the "Trisker" (CD 3) emphasizes a rhythmic give and
take that musicians call rubato, reminiscent of the sense of forward motion followed by broadening that one can hear in the way violinists approached classical music in the early twentieth century. Her aesthetic
stance brings up more issues about the classical-folk relationship than
does Svigals's work. Though Svigals acknowledges (in the quote above) the
skills her classical training contributes, she thinks of it more in terms of
enabling a certain technical freedom to move around on the violin than
as a component of affect. Svigals constantly credits her "folk" teachers
and Mediterranean sound and downplays the classical component of
klezmer, a contested issue among klezmer aficionados and artists. We
know that by the late nineteenth century, klezmorim viewed classical violin style as a higher plane of music-making, or at least as a key to upward
mobility. Beregovski tells us that small-town fiddlers subscribed to sheet
music from nearby cities to gain some rudiments. He mentions and presents concert pieces that famous klezmorim might perform at the com-
mand of the local Polish gentry for a concert at the manor house. Surely

the arpeggios that Tarras introduces bespeak a classical influence, as does much of the work of the very influential, last old-style klezmer violinist from Eastern Europe, Leon Schwartz (1901–1989).

With Deborah Strauss, the classicizing instinct is not just a matter of her technical preparation, since she has adapted to core klezmer repertoire style admirably, but also an issue of affect. While teaching, Strauss says things like, "There's tremendous beauty in being able to hold back the first time you do a phrase, then open it up the next time," or "Establish the melody, then do the ornament," or "Play everything a little more detached." Explaining one spot, she says, "If you do the rush forward" on an arpeggio, then you have to "land slow" on the cadence. A striking moment in the lesson comes when she feels she has to modify her own recorded version, which Rachel is playing exactly as she heard it. In the B section of the tune the first phrase has a repeated gesture. For the recording, Strauss's sense of the affect led her to slide three times on the D–C downward move (ex 5.6), but two years later she "can't stand" the way she played the passage and urges Rachel to maybe slide once but then do the phrasing with a different bowing, another nod to a "classical" affect in the more general sense of the word.

This sensibility also comes across as she transmits the technique of the krekhts. The modern krekhts is not easy to teach. You have to learn to stop the bow on a note, then flick an upper finger (Strauss prefers the fourth) above the pitch. "You use the pad of the finger. Not so little so it doesn't squeak at all, and not so much that it's a real note," but you produce something in between: a moan, a sigh, a sob—which is what krekhts means in Yiddish. A related word for this gesture is *kneytsh*, which means a pinch, an even more incisive metaphor. Kneytsh also has rich resonance among Yiddish speakers, even today, being a word Hasidic Jews in Jerusalem use to describe the distinctive sound of their prayer leader's chanting (Moshe Taube, personal communication). When I learned the krekhts/kneytsh from Alicia Svigals, she said ruefully, "I taught you that in five minutes, and it took me five years to figure out." Once you learn the krekhts, you feel like playing it on every other note—it's violinistic and expressive. Strauss warns Rachel about this moment: "You're going to go through a stage where you are going to want to put them anywhere . . . they're delightful things. And you should. And then you'll get to the next stage . . . where you

Example 5.6. Deborah Strauss, section 2 of "Trisker."

say, 'That's not really making music with it,' and you start pulling back." During an interview, Strauss also came around to this topic:

> An old mandolin player that Jeff [Warschauer, her husband, also a klezmer] worked with said: "You young people, you do too many *dreydlakh*" [a Yiddish term for elaborate ornamentation, often applied to cantorial singing]. There really is a tendency to sort of overornament things. . . . There's refinement that comes when you feel when they choose not to krekhts. . . . I feel the krekhtsn [plural] better than I feel the trills. There is a vocabulary, and even with our scanty resources we can piece it together.
>
> When I first started doing this, I didn't do any sliding at all . . . I thought that if you slurped around and trilled, then that was Jewish music, so I really avoided them [slides]. You can't let the ornament overtake the melody. (Interview, 1997)

This is what I am calling a "classicizing" aesthetic, referring to old attitudes like that of C.P.E. Bach's in 1753: "Above all, a prodigal use of embellishments must be avoided. Regard them as spices which may ruin the best dish or gewgaws which may deface the most pefect building" (Bach 1949:81). But I do not mean to reference Deborah Strauss's approach in the literal sense of classical violin technique. Rather there are other shadings of classicism literally in play here: an urge to trim back excessive sentimentality or showiness in the service of a restrained, deeply felt performance, and a drive to find a central set of organizing principles to stabilize a modern klezmer style. This attitude both coincides with and diverges from Svigals's approach; the reader can make his or her own comparison from the recorded examples. What should be evident by now is the deep investment the current tradition of klezmer masters makes in so-called ornament as a core of personal identity and artistic profile.

Klezmer is not alone in its intense concentration on detail. Writing about folk-based Yugoslav popular music of the 1980s, Ljerka Rasmussen isolates the trill as a key factor in registering the degree of "orientalism" that placed a singer and song inside or outside of acceptable social boundaries: "The temptation to indulge in trills was always present for Paldum [a star singer], each recording becoming an exercise in self-discipline: not to cross the line between moderation and excess . . . this involved a sensitivity to local distinctions related to melodic range and frequency of trill use" (Rasmussen 1999). As quotations from Strauss and Svigals show, it is precisely on "the line between moderation and excess" that klezmer musicians walk warily on a tightrope of taste. But a sharp distinction between the Yugoslav and klezmer cases calls us back to the special status of klezmer, unmoored from a local, even dangerous, social discourse. As we know from the fate of Yugoslavia in the 1990s, the trill was just the tiniest tip of the iceberg of distrust and potential for national separatism that would lead to major tragedy, while in the klezmer world, taste as identity remains within a limited arena of the aesthetic or the "ethnic" as personal and social play.

Within that world, though, a gesture like the krekhts takes on considerable importance as a barometer of personal and social distinction. This diacritical marking on a pitch has obviously become a hallmark of a revivalist sensibility. At the least, it is a technical hurdle and an aesthetic requirement for klezmer competence. A "scientific" analysis of the ontology of the krekhts might be in order here, using sonograms, pictures of sound events generated by computer software. With the kind assistance of Fredric Lieberman (University of California at Santa Cruz, using Soundscope) and Scott Wilson (Wesleyan University, using Lemur), it became possible to generate sonograms that act as family portraits of the klezmer krekhts. We sampled a krekhts from pioneer klezmer Abe Schwartz, from his 1925 recording of a gas-nign melody (discussed later), and then from performances of the same tune by Svigals and Strauss, so as to keep the musical context as similar as possible. As a control, we added a krekhts from Max Leibowitz, slightly earlier than Schwartz, for the older style. Figure 5.1 offers Wilson's snapshots of the krekhts.

Reading sonograms can be an impressionistic exercise, since the data, seemingly so precise, actually produce a rather cryptic projection on paper. It is also very hard to filter out the noise made by accompanying instruments, or the hiss and rumble of old recordings, from the precise sound you're trying to analyze. Even at best, the ringing of the violin's body can create acoustic complexity, so a complete phenomenology of the krekhts awaits much more intensive research and the advent of better software. A tentative reading does suggest that the two younger violinists, Svigals and Strauss, are not producing the same pitch profile as the old masters, Schwartz and Leibowitz. The former are producing a sound event that graphs very much like the way they describe it when teaching: a sonic sigh that comes from quickly putting down a finger somewhere above the note just played, just after the bow is suddenly stopped. The upper finger is not pressed down so hard that a "clean" sound it produces, and it is not lifted off the string so far as to make that ghostly violinism, the "harmonic," but the finger lies somewhere in between, mid-pressured. Lemur, as interpreted by Scott Wilson, describes the result as being "an octave and a major third plus a quarter tone above" the previous note, so "constitutes something of a mystery" as played by Strauss. His guess is that what she does physically has the effect of "cutting out the odd modes of vibration" of the string, visibly absent in the sonogram's yawning spaces where the krehts happens. Svigals's krekhts, though sounding just as evanescent as

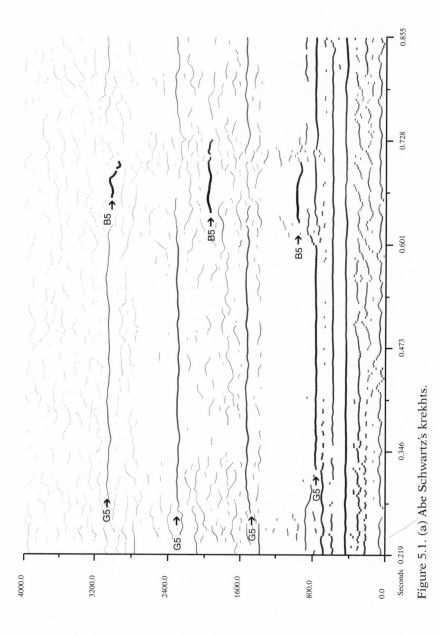

Figure 5.1. (a) Abe Schwartz's krekhts.

114

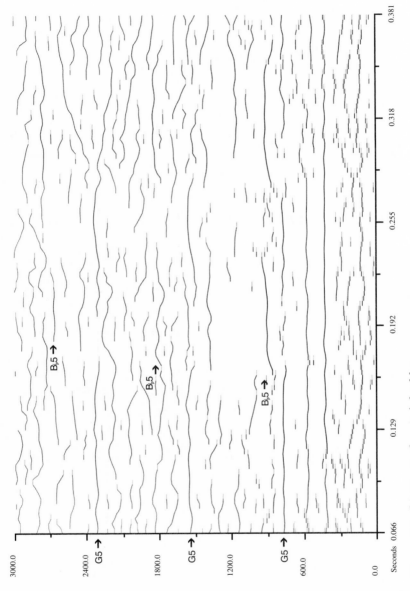

Figure 5.1. (b) Max Leibowitz's krekhts.

115

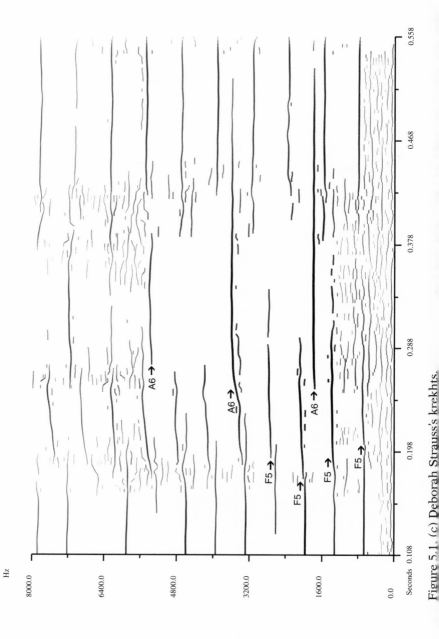

Figure 5.1. (c) Deborah Strauss's krekhts.

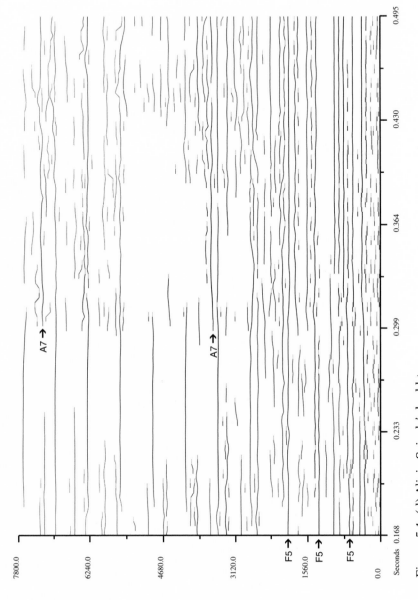

Figure 5.1. (d) Alicia Svigals's krekhts.

117

Strauss's, rings more like a "harmonic" of the fingered pitch, outlining a pitch with greater precision, at about two octaves and a third higher.

What unites Svigals and Strauss is that they differ from the "classic" krekhts of Schwartz and Leibowitz, according to the sonograms. The old-timers seem to offer distances from the fundamental pitch that look more in line with regularly occurring overtones, unfolding at approximately a third above the fundamental (G). It looks like they produce them as fingered grace notes, not the "semi-harmonics" favored by the younger players. Schwartz shows no sign of stopping the bow before playing the krekhts, yet this is the basis of the technique taught by the younger masters to their students.

What does all this mean? No one can say for sure, because of the leeway in interpreting sonograms, and the fact that we selected but a tiny sample of the available krekhts moves in the recorded klezmer violin repertoire. But these preliminary findings do suggest that the modern krekhts is a cousin to, not a twin of, the older sigh. Training one's fingers to shape sounds one has never actually seen produced involves a particular type of imaginative leap that the contemporary klezmer world constantly makes. The krekhts as perfected by modern masters like Strauss and Svigals is a bridge across an abyss of memory, spanning the Holocaust and Americanization with the smallest, most delicate stopping of the string and flicking of the finger. Perhaps the new krekhts echoes Svigals's remark about her tone color: "If klezmer fiddlers weren't doing this before, maybe they should have been." This is a form of sonic commentary on older texts that taps into deep veins of collective memory while outlining stages of personal development.

These two performers' approach to one area of ornamentation suggest just how complex a component of music-making this supposedly innocuous parameter really is, and how it combines the technical, the aesthetic, and the national. Indeed, the word "ornament" seems a remarkably impoverished way to approach the multidimensional resonance of the krekhts. Leopold Auer, an early twentieth-century contemporary of Abe Schwartz, was the great teacher who was most responsible for shifting Russian klezmer energy into classical channels. Auer has this to say in his teaching manual: "This whole question of embellishment is an obscure one, and we have still to develop an authoritative body of rules which may serve as a guide to teacher and pupil. Now as in days gone by, the use of ornament in violin playing is taught in accordance with the individual teacher's point of view, and embellishments are played as the individual player's artistic good sense may dictate" (Auer 1921:125). He might be writing about today's klezmer violin world, where teachers, along with enshrined recordings, lay down principles, leaving the rest to "artistic good sense."

Auer's approach needs extension, in an era when teachers might be disembodied recordings, voices of bygone ancestors who have left repeatable traces of their art. Here Paul Berliner's description of how young jazz musicians find their way is resonantly relevant: "Disciplined practice to master the instant absorption and reproduction of phrases from recorded solos also cultivates the ability to precisely imagine ideas and immediately recreate them. In a sense, this call and response interaction with idols on recordings represents a general model for the very process of improvising in which soloists must constantly respond to their own phrases, whether repeating them or transforming them" (Berliner 1994:199).

For klezmer, Berliner's insight needs filling out in the area that is our main topic here: the national narrative of Yiddish music. The art historians cited earlier raised "the notion, first expressed in ancient times, that there was a moral dimension to the use of ornaments." Outside of the extreme cases like Yugoslavia, already mentioned, modern heritage musics offer two possible moralities, both centered on authenticity, in two senses of the term. In its technical meaning, authenticity is available to all and serves as a benchmark of morality in the sense of propriety. Here the question would be posed the way Statman and Epstein put it: Is the ornament in the right place? The other idea of authenticity, encoded in that slippery and sentimental word "identity," carries the morality of essentialism. What Epstein, the old insider, means by "You can't teach it" is something like "I grew up with it naturally in the original milieu and played with the best of them." Statman, by talking about "a door opening to the heart of the melody," links morality to music in a different essentialist way, by making a claim of true, esoteric knowledge, probably flowing from his pilgrim-like exploration of and personal commitment to Hasidic melodic sources.

Strauss and Svigals position themselves neither as outsiders nor as pilgrims, but as committed, seeking, individualistic musicians. Their position on ornaments might be closer to that of C. P. E. Bach (1949:79) when he says, "Without them the best melody is empty and ineffective, the clearest content clouded." For them, the morality of ornament is effectiveness and clarity combined with personal statement, but not without an interest in the narrative to which they belong, especially now that they do so much teaching.

I think a broader consideration of ornament and identity could stretch across most of the Euro-American heritage musics being played today, from Irish to Balkan and beyond. Even the smallest flexible unit of such systems can suggest a range of interpretation from the personal to the national, with each moment compressing simultaneous systems of loss and rediscovery. A final note on ornament can take us back to its ancient roots: as part of rhetoric, the necessary persuasion that an orator, or a musician,

needs to make his or her case. Writing two thousand years ago, Quintillian made a point of including ornament in explaining rhetoric: "The
speaker who possesses it fights not merely with effective, but with flash-
ing weapons . . . the flash of the sword in itself strikes something of terror
to the eye . . . for when our audience find it a pleasure to listen, their
attention and their readiness to believe what they hear are both alike in-
creased" (Quintillian 1922:213; my thanks to Peter Hoyt for this quotation). Quintillian's fascinating linkage of the persuasive power of orna-
mental pleasure through its sheer flash resonates with today's klezmer
aesthetic, and his metaphoric allusion to the terror of the sword's glint
alerts us to the seriousness that ornament can imply.

Types of ornament can be very instrument-specific, as in the case of the
sword, so we need to extend the violinistic turn of this discussion to include vibrato, another hot topic among klezmer fiddlers. Walter Zev Feldman feels that vibrato infiltrated the klezmer world slowly, with the advent of classical music into Eastern European Jewish circles, so should be
minimized in reconstructive performance today. Strauss agrees, telling
her student Rachel, who as a classically trained violinist is using a great
deal of vibrato instinctively, to reduce this type of expressivity: "It's not
that for the rest of your klezmer-playing life you won't use vibrato, but you
need to quiet it down; you add it as needed. It's good for you to start with
a clean palette as opposed to a classical vibrato." To some extent, this is
an American aesthetic, arising from the stress on purity of style among a
large number of tightly interacting klezmorim. In Europe, where the
klezmer phenomenon is newer, more isolated, or even embattled, the need
for expression may be understood differently, as Leon Pollak of Vienna
commented. He fell out with Joshua Horowitz, an important American-
born musician who was his partner, partly over issues of "authenticity,"
including the vibrato issue. "Maybe in the countryside, in the Ukraine or
elsewhere, they played without vibrato, but in time there was an opening,
a social one, and they heard other music, so they learned vibrato." But it
is not this historical argument that moves him toward endorsing the affect of this technique. "Everyday problems, worries, and joys were all reflected in the music, so when we come to the perspective of vibrato or not
vibrato, it has to do with many emotions, many experiences, and destinies, heavy destinies" (interview, 1997).

The point is that technique is inseparable from an affect the player assumes about the piece, and that the affect flows from deeper aesthetic as-
sumptions that are informed by questions ranging from the history of early
klezmer through the meaning of Jewish music. Overarching the whole
process is the musician's need to find an individual credo, extracted from
a necessary sense of genealogy that is filtered through a set of personal temperament and life experiences. But there is no need to romanticize this

process: it proceeds in the pressured context of the relationships among band members and between bands and audiences. The interlinked factors offered earlier—musical magnetism, marketing, the power of evocation—impact technique implicitly and explicitly. Neither side of the equation, the personal or the social, predominates, both being reflected in the technical decision-making detailed for just one tune, "Dem Trisker Rebns Khosid." Any given performance by Dave Tarras was just as contingent; unfortunately, no one interviewed him in 1925 to map the semantic field around his playing. Rather, the aura of his work continues to radiate, its energy harnessed by sound recording, available at any moment to inspire improvisation born of emulation. It is in this sense that modern American performances by highly sensitive and experienced artists like Svigals or Strauss seem to function as Jewish commentary on secular texts that have became artistically sacred and socially valuable in our times across a large listenership and among many musicians.

Yet another version of the "Trisker" tune brings home the style layers that coexist in any particular variant of a long-lived item. Just when Svigals was recording her "Trisker" in 1996, the Toronto group Flying Bulgar Klezmer Band was in the studio producing theirs (CD 5). The liner notes simply refrence Tarras as their original inspiration. The Bulgar's performance begins with a solo violin, then allows trumpet, accordion, and trumpet to take up the melody line. This more chamber-like formation has been filtering into recent klezmer albums. It seems groups want to skip past the leader-centered New York 78s of the "golden age" and return to what they feel must have been the more collective style of pre-recording klezmer. They keep the Tarras beat but relax it just a shade, and end with their own slowed-down farewell section. The band stays quite faithful to many of Tarras's signature turns of phrase and his overall approach to tune-building. For the occasion, they brought in Steve Greenman on the violin. Greenman grew up in Cleveland, where he honed his fiddle skills playing in Central European bar bands and, though Jewish, came late to klezmer. He studied with Svigals, and her trademark timbral tension marks his soulful playing. This "Trisker," then, sounds like a marriage of Tarras and Svigals, nicely highlighting the multisource nature of today's versions of yesterday's tunes.

Since that album, Greenman has been studying klezmer style with Walter Zev Feldman, who practices a rather austere philosophy of authenticity. Steeped in scholarship about klezmer roots, Feldman has formed a band called Khevrisa (an alternate Yiddish term for "band" from the more common *kapelye*) that aims at fidelity to a nineteenth-century sound. This experimentation with affect through instrumental technique is nothing new in klezmer, but each new attempt to break the standard molds comes as a refreshing surprise in the ongoing process of revitalization.

BEFORE LEAVING "Dem Trisker Rebns Khosid," it is worth looking back at Dave Tarras, who recorded a different version of the piece at the end of his career, when he was being rediscovered both by young klezmorim and by an older audience that had not heard him for many years. In 1978, 53 years after first recording this durable piece, at the age of 81 he played it again as part of the historic Balkan Arts Center "klezmer renaissance" project; it was his last recording. Here he was accompanied just by his longtime associates, Sam Beckerman on accordion and Irving Graetz on drums. The piece is now called "Ba dem Zeydns Tish," "At Grandfather's Table," accurately referencing Tarras's original contact with the nign that inspired his recordings (CD 4). The 1978 version is so truncated and so different from the 1925 recording that it takes a while to recognize the similarity. Tarras is clearly not the "klezmer king" of the old days, and he does only section 1 of the tune he did in 1925, adding other parts of different klezmer stock melodies. This "Trisker" has the distinct sound of an actual wedding performance; indeed, the whole album is structured as a look back at the klezmer's night at the nuptials. Graetz plays a rock-steady, stiff dance beat, and Beckerman constantly fills in for the probably weary Tarras. Interestingly, Tarras does a lot more arpeggio movement in the tune than in 1925, playing standard phrases rather than adventurously improvising. What James Cowdery (1990:122–33), studying Irish traditional music, has called "recombining" melody segments in folk tune performance has scarcely been discussed for the klezmer repertoire. The liner notes say merely: "Though most of these melodies had not been a part of his active repertoire for decades, Tarras seemed completely at home with them," hardly surprising given the number of years he played pieces like the "Trisker." It is worth rehearsing once again the oft-repeated tale of how, at this point in the late 1970s, Andy Statman and Walter Zev Feldman coaxed Dave Tarras into playing the old tunes, which from his point of view represented a music that was outdated and irrelevant.

I have chosen this performance to close the section on "Dem Trisker Rebns Khosid" not so much to show what a 53-year gap does to a master musician, but to give some sense of the more everyday, humdrum style of play that has always typified the klezmer's weekly rounds of making a living, as opposed to the intense, searching exploration that musicians like Svigals and Strauss are making into the subtleties and nuances of the style, much of which they learned from the inspired live performance moments that the recording studio instigated. The routine, workmanlike production of a micromusic still goes on when klezmorim play for parties, but it tends to be masked by the carefully engineered versions that make up the albums we rely upon for evaluating and analyzing current klezmer practice. Style, though conventional, is never unitary at any point in the history of a tune, a player, or a tradition.

Case Study 2: The "Gas-nign"

This tune has had a long and distinguished recorded history and can stretch the analytical insights gained from "Dem Trisker Rebns Khosid" just a bit further. Rather than view the piece in process of change, I would like to present a more synchronic set of snapshots from the klezmer family album. Much the same approach is common to European folk music studies in general, such as the British ballad (Bronson 1969) or the Irish melody (Cowdery 1990). For some reason, klezmer music has not attracted the same level of intense scrutiny. Klezmorim have been coming to grips with the same stylistic issues repeatedly over the generations. Those issues are posed by the structure of cherished tunes, beautifully crafted cultural artifacts that suit and embody the folk aesthetic of the Eastern European Jews.

A *gas-nign* is a "street tune," but it was not just a tune played by street musicians; rather, it was part of the wedding ritual cycle. Klezmorim sounded it into the streets as the wedding party moved from one house to another, along the prescribed stages of what was often a multiday event. A gas-nign, then, is a genre, a package of well-understood musical conventions that involve function and form. The function was completely lost in the recording studio, never to be regained. People didn't carry their gramophones through the streets, nor did they transmit the tradition of complex social choreography that would require a gas-nign. So this particular gas-nign survives as a particularly attractive tune, divorced from its older context.

That survival depends on the musical profile: a lovely tune in two parts that is one example of a type: the "slow hora " or *zhok*, depending on where you come from in southeastern Europe. Walter Zev Feldman feels that the stimulus for this type of Jewish tune came from non-Jewish Moldavian sources sometime in the nineteenth century. What captivates listeners today♪ about the slow hora is the basic insistent, redolent rhythm: ♪♩♪ in staff notation, perceived as ONE-rest-THREE ONE-rest-THREE ONE, or simply NOTE-silence-NOTE-NOTE-silence, and so on. Kurt Bjorling and his colleagues in the band Brave Old World use this "Gas-nign" as a teaching piece for their transatlantic workshops; Bjorling thinks of the rhythm as forming a five-beat unit. In any case, it is the silence, the hesitation that most players bring to the pause between pitches, that gives the slow hora its charm. While it might be descended from, and related to, co-territorial musics, in America and in today's klezmer world this genre spells Jewishness and evokes an "old country" sound.

Listening to variants of this gas-nign from the early and later phases of klezmer recording offers a rich array of possibilities for personal statement, since musicians can rely on its core affect. (Not all versions discussed here are on the accompanying CD, because of permissions issues.) One early version that has been highly influential is that of bandleader Abe Schwartz, who called his version "National Hora" and who recorded it in 1920 on violin, accompanied by what on the sheet music was called "the famous pianist his daughter Miss Schwartz" (CD 6). Two points about this packaging deserve mention. The first is the piano accompaniment. This is atypical for European klezmer performance, the piano being a middle-class instrument not readily available to many traditional musicians and certainly not natural in contexts of weddings or, more precisely here, street music, which demand flexibility and portability. So we are witnessing a move toward upward mobility and Americanization. The domestic femininity of the young woman accompanist, who is even the violinist's daughter, underlines the piano's role in the culture of the day. Immigrants were sold pianos on a massive basis as part of their socialization into American life, with the daughters getting the lessons (Slobin 1982:44–46). The second point Schwartz's version raises arises from the title of the piece. No longer a gas-nign, as the piano arrangement implies, the piece as national hora sends a new social signal. "Hora" is a Romanian genre, while "national" implies "Jewish" here; the combination of the two words in an American context provides a certain narrative about identity, grounding it in a European tradition while staking out an ethnic enclave.

Around the same time, Jacob "Jakie" Hoffman also recorded the gas-nign with Kandel's band (CD 7). Hoffman was one of the figures Hankus Netsky has studied in the Philadelphia klezmer context. Not only a wedding musician, Hoffman, as xylophonist, was active in the Philadelphia Orchestra and the Ballets Russe touring company. Using a classical music instrument, Hoffman's rendition of the gas-nign relies on a rock-steady brass backup that gives the soloist a chance to stand out in relief with a staccato line that manages miraculously to preserve the ornamentation pattern of the older klezmer core repertoire.

Earlier Max Weissman's 1920 recording of the gas-nign was mentioned as an example of the frustration we feel when we hear a single side of a klezmer master about whom we know nothing. Weissman's performance is sinuous, chromatic at points where no one else chooses that way of moving through the tune (CD 8). He loves the low register and projects something of a southeastern European, perhaps Greek sound, that is far from both Schwartz's fairly precise violinistics and Hoffman's pearly xylophonism. Perhaps Weissman's distinctive sound explains why his discography is limited to one item: according to the side's listing in the Spottswood catalogue of ethnic recordings (1990), the performance was "recorded as a Victor trial," a test that the clarinetist apparently flunked. There is a recorded version by Leon Schwartz (1901–1989), the only violin mentor from the old days of klezmer, whose sound became available to younger players in his last years. Other effective and eye-opening versions of the gas-nign include two from the days of LP recordings somewhere in the 1950s to 1960s, one zfeaturing veteran player Howie Leese and the other Max Epstein, who won the 1998 National Heritage Fellowship of the National Endowment for the Arts (CD 13). The Viennese musician Leon Pollak offered me a live recording of the piece he made in Prague (CD 10). Alicia Svigals has a stunning version on her *Fidl* album (CD 12). I have also elicited spontaneous performances during interviews as "laboratory samples," to yield completely unpolished, intuitive performances, and one such spontaneous version by Deborah Strauss is included in the analysis of the piece (CD 11).

David Krakauer's "Gas-nign" of 1999, presented here from a live performance at Tonic, currently the hottest klezmer venue in New York, offers a different kind of personal statement, one from within the klezmer circle (CD 14). Krakauer's vision is far from reverential revivalists' variants of the tune. Krakauer "follows the form," as he says (interview, 1999), but overlays the A and B section repeats with his own design: a radical rise from the clarinet's low register to its high range, followed by a return to the opening sound, which now sounds intensely defamiliarized. This gas-nign is the closing item on Krakauer's tribute to the great New Orleans clarinetist Sidney Bechet, and while not part of the Bechet suite on the album *New York Klezmer,* the streetwise playing, overlaying an almost parade-like drumbeat with soaring sounds and a reflective reprise of the melody, suggests an intricate interplay of older and New York sensibilities, tinged by the overlap of New Orleans that Krakauer suggests when he says "Every note I play on the clarinet is informed by Sidney Bechet in terms of timbre and attack" (interview, 1999).

To show the full range of possibilities this lovely tune offers musicians, I have included a solo piano version of the "Gas-nign" by Ran Blake, a renowned improviser at the New England Conservatory who has been inspired by the long-term klezmer presence there (CD 15). Blake brings his whole creative arsenal to bear on a tune designed to do very different work. Here is a description of what he was thinking:

> It starts with anger. We are in Europe after the war, and remembering a film noir sort of scene (perhaps the scene in *The Pawnbroker* where the mother, father, son, and daughter are all together as the Nazi troops come in). In the middle, there's a cry against repression (reminiscent of "Let My People Go"), and then, since it's a survivor looking back, a mixture of hope and nostalgia. There's a controlled kind of drama here, and some American elements too: gospel underpinnings and an appearance by Thelonius Monk. (interview with Hankus Netsky, 1999)

Figure 5.2. Joseph Hoffman's manuscript version of Gas-nign, 1926.

Rather than analyzing countless variants of the gas-nign in depth, though such as study would make a serious contribution to our understanding of klezmer style, I will focus on just one phrase from a few performances to open a window onto klezmer style from the point of view of the choices musicians make, continuing the topic of compositional logic. Overall, this gas-nign has an elegant design, in two parts, each with subsections. Figure 5.2 gives the standardized version of the tune as notated in 1926 by Joseph Hoffman, father of Jacob Hoffman, for the Philadelphia klezmer circle. He calls it "Rumanian Horry" (= "hora"). Somewhat original in notation, with its apostrophe-like natural signs, the old klezmer notates the tune in the standardized sheet-music version of 3/8 for the slow hora. Hoffman's variant carefully includes some "ornaments"—trills and grace notes—showing once again that even when notating a skeletal version to be fleshed out in performance, he feels he must include the little turns and twists that give the tune its flavor.

The gas-nign tune unfolds with parallelisms, presenting a melodic line made up of matching and contrasting gestures. Section 1 consists of two subsections (marked A and B in figure 5.2), the first of which is made up of phrases that begin the same way (marked "a" and "b"), setting out the idea of parallelism. In section 2, the design of subsections with parallel phrasing returns, as shown by the repeated A-A-A figure in the first and third measures of the section, and then in repetitions of rhythmically similar small units that themselves consist of repeated measures marked by Hoffman's "repeat-this-measure" markings (✗). The gas-nign's interest in recognizability offers very different solutions than did the "Trisker" tune, which featured identical cadences and line endings. This type of tune logic suggests that the tradition has a strong need for orderliness and easily identifiable patterning, but also an intense interest in blazing many trails to this same aesthetic destination.

The point selected for a zoom-in analysis is in section 2. This section begins in the high register. Its subsection a (beginning where section 2 does) is almost completely interested in a single pitch (here transcribed as the note "A"), approached repeatedly from below, then above, with different flourishes. Subsection b beginning at X unfolds a descending line from the A down to the tonal center, D, featuring a repeated gesture in a kind of terraced downward motion in two parallel stages; it is on this moment of melodic flow that we will focus (ex. 5.7). For convenience, the reiterated descending units will be labeled X and Y, and the internal repetitions will be labeled X-1, X-2 and Y-1, Y-2. The tune makes its demands, and musicians comply, but they add their individual voice as a response. Each of the musicians over the past seventy years included in a small survey here makes different decisions about how to play X and Y. Their choices can be framed as a set of answers to the following implicit questions:

Should the musician play X-1 and X-2 (or Y-1 and Y-2) the same way or differently?

Should the musician play X and Y with the same gesture pattern, or interpret them differently?

Should X's and Y's rhythmic outline be syncopated or regular?

Should any of the notes be marked by diacritics—the little turns, trills, and krekhts of the klezmer sound? If so, which ones, and on which notes should they fall?

Should the musician use long notes to outline the basic pitches of the melody, or subdivide them into mini-articulations of shorter notes?

Should the musician play X and Y the same way every time the B section comes around, or find new solutions (as Alicia Svigals does) for each repetition?

Example 5.7 lays out the answers a particular set of musicians has made to these stylistic questions. Clearly, there is no "right" or "traditional" way

Example 5.7. Gas-nign detail showing individual variation. For sources, see "Contents of Accompanying CD," except for: Howie Leese, performance of unknown date and album loaned to author; Leon Schwartz, from listening to *Leon Schwartz: "Like in a Different World,"* Global Village Records C 109, 1993.

to play these small melodic units under our microscope. The placement of trills, turns, and krekhts was unpredictable, as were the decisions along the dimensions of same/different and regular/syncopated. Doubtless, each performance represents an immediate set of choices, as it did for Strauss, who played a spontaneous "laboratory" version. She talked about its arbitrariness as soon as she realized what she had played. Yet it was also clear that younger musicians had listened to older recordings and respected them. For example, Pollak takes his cue, but not his details, from Abe Schwartz. Personality comes across strongly in other parameters than just the melodic, and these are very hard to notate. One is tone color, which emerges from the player's intimate relationship to his or her chosen instrument. Another, in all slow-hora performances, is the attitude the musician takes toward the basic rhythm: How much hesitation between second and third beat? How much elasticity by the soloist against the steady backup of the band? Are the smallest melodic units to be understood as three-beat, five-beat, or larger groupings, and how long are phrases, those breath-lengths of melody? The answers to these questions specify the aesthetic and the affect of klezmorim, if not the "attitude," in the current sense of the word.

To round out this look at the meaning of style, one more case study extends the range a bit, from Feldman's "core repertoire" to his "transitional" repertoire.

Case Study 3: The "Araber-tants"

What Feldman calls the "transitional repertoire" plays a pivotal role in klezmer music. Through networks of travel and business, Eastern European musicians moved melodies across long-distance routes and picked and chose whatever they liked. A long-term process of domestication infused the Jewish repertoire with items that had originated elsewhere, geographically or ethnically. Most often, the actual patterns of derivation and metamorphosis are opaque, but sometimes the regional and ethnic overlaps are transparent. One such case is the so-called "Araber-tants." Klezmer scholar Martin Schwartz (personal communication) has seen it first as an Istanbul version from the first decade of the twentieth century; the melody is known among Greeks as a *syrto* dance tune. Somehow it made its way to Jewish circles, where someone affixed the label "Arabic" to it. The Greek and Near Eastern connection to klezmer was "particularly strong before the middle of the nineteenth century, resulting from the strong presence of Greek language and culture in Romanian cities," where klezmorim were plentiful and influential. "In America, where immigrant klezmorim had easy access to the music of the Greek community, this Near Eastern character became more pronounced once again. In fact, it was the Greek-American market that continued to support klezmer music after the Jews had largely abandoned it in the 1950s" (Feldman 1997).

At almost exactly the same time in the mid-1920s the piece was recorded by Dave Tarras and Naftule Brandwein, the two masters Feldman cites as being especially interested in the Greek/Near Eastern repertoire, for very different purposes and under different titles. Tarras, like many other klezmers of his time, played with Greek musicians. He did a series of Greek recordings in the mid-1920s as a bandleader for the "Columbia [Records] Greek Orchestra," and the piece is called "Magia Monikanes." It is the same tune that Brandwein labeled "Araber-tants." As the two versions are listened to with the exquisite hindsight of today, Tarras seems not exactly idiomatic as a Greek musician. Flashes of klezmer clarinet style peep through the facade, yet Greek-Americans did buy these discs. Brandwein, supposedly playing an Arabic dance, stamps out a strong klezmer statement for a Jewish audience through his trademark clarinetic magic (CD 16). Feldman's term "transitional" seems apt for both the European and the American contexts. The "Araber-tants" makes occasional appearances on the current klezmer circuit and is even included in a concise klezmer tunebook compiled by Hankus Netsky.

A 1996 recording by the young Berlin band La'om suggests the current European range of responses to the Tarras–Brandwein canon (CD 17). This version becomes less clearly klezmer as the beat and instrumentation morph into a tango sound. Mattias Groh's attempt at improvisatory fiddle soloing owes little to the klezmer tradition. The tune's title rings ever more ironic: the "Arabic" reference seems remarkably distant from the trail that leads the tune to East Berlin. La'om is riffing on an American product imported to Europe, even as the album evokes an old Jewish world. La'om's experience in gathering its repertoire has almost completely been from Americans. Its members proudly told me how they wangled German government funding to attend KlezKamp, and they have worked hard in klezmer workshops run by Americans in Germany. For whom and how has this *lieu de memoire* arrived on a compact disc? La'om's performance holds up a funhouse mirror reflection of Eastern Europe music-making and is all the more striking in light of the long-lasting Western European approach to Balkan and Turkish music over last twenty-five years. Young musicians coming from places like Stockholm have ransacked southeastern Europe for inspiration, playing with local bands and putting out sound-alike CDs. Yet in a more cut-off city, Berlin (especially in the eastern sector), things took a different path, particularly since Jewish materials have a special associative field, even if they're called "Arab." Weaving this ethnic patchwork ever more densely, La'om's liner notes point out that the "Araber-tants" is in the *terkish* ("Turkish") style of klezmer, a generalized term for a number of transitional repertoire items.

The continued transformations of the "Araber-tants" teach us about the way style and repertoire shift slowly, slipping out from under one heading and coming to temporary rest in the next column. This piece started life somewhere in the Balkans and moved into the Jewish world as part of a large-scale process of domestication. Once the tune migrated to New York, it found itself a home in an aesthetic neighborhood shared by Greeks and Jews. Becoming part of a new core repertoire in the 1970s, the canon of recorded "klezmer music," the "Araber-tants" could spread to Germany and elsewhere, becoming in a sense transitional once again, this time for Europeans who were reaching out to embrace a new supply of tunes and affects. For La'om, this arbitrariness is part of the joy of learning, of flexing its musical muscles and of looking for an audience. As they describe their situation to me (e-mail, June 1998), "We still are that non-simkhe quintet [i.e., not a private party band] who enjoy playing sophisticated arrangements in a not so sophisticated sounding way. We still like to pick repertoire from the rims and former neighbors of Klezmer Music—although Naftule [Brandwein] probably went even further 'out' when picking tunes for his repertoire." Notions of stylistic authenticity seem less important to the band than a search for self-expression and performance niche. The night I went to hear them in Berlin at the Bellevue, the only audience was the friends they had invited; they had strayed too far from their usual clubs. This could be the fate of klezmer over the years anywhere in Europe, since as a music system, it has shallow roots and for the most part lacks a substantial, supportive community that regularly rejoices in its presence at their celebrations. With limited exposure, fluctuating expectations, and a fragile history, the specifics of style often remain more tentative as a structuring component than overall aesthetic and the immediate affect of performance.

Thousands of miles away, near Monterey Bay, California, the band Hootza-tza thinks about the "Araber-tants" very differently. This group, whose profile appears in chapter 3 through the narrative of its violinist Laurie Tanenbaum, is made up of Santa Cruzans from very diverse musical backgrounds. They imagine the piece as having a long introductory riff of a light Mediterranean quality, and they hear the tune itself as being based on a solid Middle Eastern hand-drum sound (CD 18). Santa Cruz is a place where the city council had to pass an ordinance restricting open-air drumming, and where the sign in the window of the local world music shop says "20% off on Moroccan bongos," so it comes as no surprise that Ken Mowrey's drumbeat drives the performance. Mowrey started out as a guitarist but was slowly drawn into the percussion world, no doubt by the exuberance of the local musical environment.

These examples of the "Araber-tants" suggest the intersection of two imagined worlds: the Eastern European Jewish and the Balkan/Middle

Eastern, a historical fact that the piece's peregrinations outline more sharply than other cultural data. That resonance has a different ring in Berlin than in Santa Cruz for many geographic and historical reasons, but in both cases it is part of a general world music affect, tolerant and eclectic. I am not entirely sure what the piece meant to Tarras, Brandwein, and their mixed ethnic audience, but I do think that, in part, both the 1920s and 1990s contexts for the piece have as much to do with the fraternity and mentality of musicians as with weighty notions of memory and identity.

THE FOREGOING MINI-CASE STUDIES should merely whet the reader's appetite for close listening of klezmer music. What emerges is a remarkably consistent understanding of the basic set of resources that mark klezmer in the modern mind as a distinctive and attractive world music. Over the past eight decades, the tunes themselves have outlasted their original social function and place of origin, circulating and recirculating through the ears of audiences and the minds of musicians as portable, attractive chronotopes and soundscapes. Sometimes, when conditions are right, the tunes can actually help to reconstitute the sense of community they have outlived, a real tribute to the power of music to integrate social formations.

6

The Fiddler's Farewell

At the end of the old-time Jewish wedding, the klezmorim would strike up a good-night piece. Beregovski tells us that in Eastern Europe they often played "Zayt Gezunderheyt, Mayne Libe Eltern" ("Farewell, My Dear Parents"), a poignant reminder of the music's ability to mark the edge of the social frame. The musicians might also strike up "Es Togt Shoyn" ("Day Is Already Breaking"), which seems more addressed to the guests, notifying them that dawn brings the return of responsibility after a night of revelry. In Philadelphia the local "Good night waltz" was indispensable as signal and send-off from the catering hall. It is a lovely, minor-key parallel to the upbeat, major-key American standard "Good Night, Ladies."[1] I cannot take leave of this book so lyrically, since there are loose ends to tie up.

Those threads come together in a knotted central term that has been noticeably absent throughout: identity. Stalking horse and red herring, identity occupies a prime spot on the main roads of public discourse, and might perhaps be more aptly metaphorized as a banana peel. I have suggested some klezmer identities but would like to work through the word as a way of grappling more forcefully with klezmer's particular and peculiar nature. Here is a quote from Zygmunt Bauman, whose gift for trenchant phrasings makes him a suitable starter:

> Indeed, if the modern "problem of identity" was how to construct an identity and keep it solid and stable, the postmodern "problem of identity" is primarily how to avoid fixation and keep options open. In the case of identity, as in other cases, the catchword of modernity was creation; the catchword of postmodernity is recycling. (Bauman 1996:18)

133

Does this formulation fit the story of klezmer? Yes and no. One way to read the popularity of klezmer recordings in the 1920s, when the great wave of Jewish immigration to the United States crested, might be as a gesture toward a "solid and stable" identity in the context of sharp breaks and rapid transitions. This would suit equally well the heyday of the Yiddish theater and its musical products that I have described elsewhere (Slobin 1982). By contrast, the recent reclamation of klezmer can look like an attempt by some of today's Jewish-Americans to "keep options open," to "avoid fixation" into the role of standard postmodern consumer-citizens by finding a new context for an older identity. And yes, some of the life stories of musicians yield exquisite examples of personal "recycling."

But these supposed postmodernists also appear to be searching for something "solid and stable." Long-term commitment to the difficult life of the professional klezmer can hardly be described as mere shuffling of personae in a desperate avoidance of modernist "creation." Just the opposite occurs among current klezmorim: an urgent push toward self-creation that entails inconsistent income and ambiguous status in a business-driven, bourgeois-dominated society. The "recycling" side of identity might better fit the European context, where musicians and audiences are on the prowl for new taste sensations. Yet even here we run into the stubbornly solid and stable identity of Jewishness that informs and shapes much of the response to klezmer, especially in Central and Eastern Europe. That identity is hardly "modern," being rather another spasm of the two-millennium-long clenched embrace of Christian and Jew that succeeded the Romans' cataclysmic confrontation with the Israelites.

Another angle on identity, that of Stuart Hall, offers more leverage:

> Actually identities are about questions of using the resources of history, language and culture in the process of becoming rather than being. . . . Identities are therefore constituted within, not outside representation. . . . They arise from the narrativization of the self . . . and therefore always [are] partly constructed in fantasy, or at least within a fantasmatic field. (Hall 1996:4)

This seems closer to the nature of klezmer, a field of cultural action in which people use very specific resources of history, language, and culture in the "narrativization of the self." Hall's stress on "fantasy" and "fantasmatic" seems appropriate for the klezmer context. We have seen how the dull grind of the 1940s catering hall could not serve as springboard for the narrative-questing Jewish-American musicians of the 1970s and 1980s. Instead they turned to the romance of European origins, or at least to the musical heroics of the immigrant recorded masters. They coaxed Dave Tarras into remembering his klezmer days, ignoring his pride in having survived as a musician by learning mainstream American musics. For Europeans, any klezmer connection is rife with fantasy, since almost no non-Jews still alive on that continent at the turn of the millennium have seen a klezmer band in its full-blooded pre-Stalinist/pre-Hitlerian context. In this sense, identity is a comfortable blanket under which to tuck an uncounted and indeterminate set of stimuli and responses to the soundscape and semantic field of klezmer. As Alan Bern simply puts it about the whole range of Euro-klezmer, "Everyone is looking for meaning" (interview, 1997).

Stuart Hall insists on a particular poststructuralist reading of identity that goes just a bit further and bears on the klezmer question:

> Above all, and directly contrary to the form in which they are constantly invoked, identities are constructed through, not outside difference. This entails the radically disturbing recognition that it is only through the relation to the Other, the relation to what it is not, to precisely what it lacks, to what has been called its constitutive outside that the "positive" meaning of any terms—and thus its "identity"—can be constructed. (ibid.:4)

So the "fantasy" is not about an identity you discover inside yourself, which might provide an easy narrative, but rather it represents a response to coming up empty-handed in searching through the pockets of the self. This view moves Hall closer to that postmodernism Bauman invokes. If we like, we can read some, perhaps most klezmer scenes and products this way. Conveniently, klezmer was simply invisible for decades, so until about 1990, it was part of a missing Other. Once noticed along personal pathways, klezmer can now be picked up and wielded as a machete to hack through the underbrush of postmodernity (or is it the debris of modernity?).

But is there a single identity? Current identity discourse says no:

> . . . identities are never unified and, in late modern times, increasingly fragmented and fractured; never singular but multiply constructed across different, often intersecting and antagonistic, discourses, practices and positions. They are subject to a radical historicization, and are constantly in the process of change and transformation (ibid.).

Of course. Klezmer musicians, klezmerphiles, and accidental listeners are all "multiply constructed." This explains the moving in and out of activism or habitual listening, the clear sense of klezmer as a wave that may be cresting. No one is a unitary, old-time klezmer born into a caste-like crowd of professional musicians and fated to wander the back roads of Europe or to turn up every week at the same American catering hall to play for a succession of interchangeable weddings. Still, we need to specify the particular form of "radical historicization" that has gotten us to the current klezmer moment, since it took seismic action to reach this point.

For modern Jews, identity has been increasingly fragmented and fractured since the beginning of modernity. In the late nineteenth century, klezmer was already located on the fault line of cultural earthquake country, site of "intersecting and antagonistic discourses." Poised between Hasidic and normative ritual life, between the folk and the pop worlds of the home and the theater, acting as a trafficker of non-Jewish tunes and dance steps, the klezmer's work can stand as symbol of a delicate balance of culture, perhaps a tightrope walk across the chasm of modernity. More down to earth, one is reminded of the New York Hasidic wedding, where the band is positioned between the men's and women's versions of *simkhe*, or rejoicing. On the men's side, the black-coated, conscientious celebrants try to maintain what they think are the old folkways of their forefathers. Set off by a screen, on the women's side, you can see country western line dancing or whatever is fashionable "on the outside," since severe gender restriction allows for unseen improvisation, though not to let down your hair literally. These paradoxes of modernism have infiltrated the supposedly closed world of the Orthodox. In secular society, they even more piercingly penetrate and suffuse the concert hall and the record store, circulate in the rehearsal spaces of bands, and enrich the choices made by managers and booking agents.

We cannot claim too much for klezmer. As a system, it receded in times of cultural danger. Unlike the redemptive or at least compensatory role David Roskies (1984) describes for Jewish literature, klezmer was never a refuge, a sanctuary of identity in a storm of historical contingency. But in its attractive and persuasive way, klezmer might be part of a process Lawrence Grossberg identifies, or at least hopes for, when he tries to mark out a space for "belonging" rather than identity, for common action rather than the overdetermined "resistance" and opposition beloved of cultural studies analysis:

> It is only at the intersection of the various lines at the concrete place of belonging that we can identify . . . new modes of individuation and even subjectivation with no identity. Such a community would be based only on the exteriority, the exposure, of the singularity of belonging. A politics of singularity would need to define places people can belong to or, even more fundamentally, places people can find their way to. (Grossberg 1996:104)

Many people on both sides of the Atlantic and in the far-flung satellites of Euro-American culture from South Africa to Australia have seen klezmer as a place they could discover, if not inhabit. What has happened to klezmer in recent times is that an ever-increasing number of people, coming from many directions and with many motivations, continue to "find their way" to it. It is as a sound, a style, and sometimes even a vision of community that klezmer uniquely brings together a cluster of affects, a selection of sentiments with a hint of memory. Having gone this far with Grossberg, we must part ways; klezmer is not going to become a site of spontaneous, large-scale political activity, the hoped-for goal of his "singularity."

A more modest cultural politics emerges from a subtle substratum of sensibilities, a structure of feeling rather than a platform for action. Klezmer is having its moment as an attractive and accepted form of ethnic expressivity in the United States and, to some extent, in various parts of the new Europe. Simultaneously, it has marked out a modest niche as a transnational music resource, an opening that it might lose or widen. It would be going too far to describe the klezmer scene with the postmodern term "neo-tribe," but even if we did, we would have to note what Zygmunt Bauman says about such social formations:

> "Membership" is relatively easily revocable, and it is divorced from long-term obligations . . . neo-tribes "exist" solely by individual decisions to sport the symbolic tags of tribal allegiance. They vanish once the decisions are revoked or the zeal and determination of "members" fades out. They persevere only thanks to their continuing seductive capacity. They cannot outlive their power of attraction. (Bauman 1992:136–37)

Music systems powerful enough to suggest neo-tribalism tend to be more visible and commodified than klezmer will ever be. Lack of visibility can allow a certain sustainable niche for a small micromusic, the way a proto-bird might have watched the dinosaurs move toward oblivion. For its core audience of people who take Eastern European Jewish culture seriously, klezmer will maintain the seductive power that has brought so many younger musicians under its spell. For those listeners and players who have been brought into the fold only as browsers, "neo-tribal" membership will indeed be short-lived, but their place will be taken by still newer fans making "individual decisions" to enjoy—or possibly to play—the music, or even to take on the klezmer lifestyle. For the forseeable future, there will always be fiddlers on the move.

Notes

1. Under the Klezmer Umbrella

1. After this book went to press, the first two book-length studies of klezmer came out, Ottens and Rubin 1999 and Sapoznik 1999, which I did not have time to take account of here.

2. Klezmer as a Heritage Music

1. Netsky also says that the producers of the anniversary show told him they would show the diva Jessye Norman standing at the pinnacle of Masada, the sacred historic site, and asked him what she should sing. The arbitrary nature of the signs here is impressive.

2. Unfortunately, the available literature that might cover this topic tends to step around it. Work on the American cultural influence in Europe (e.g., Dean and Gabilliet 1996, Kroes 1996) stays within the orbit of popular culture trends; and studies of local adaptation of transnational musics (Mitchell 1996), while critiquing the too generalized notion of "cultural imperialism," also stick to the tried and true circuit of mass-appeal musical styles, the "rock, pop, and rap" of Mitchell's subtitle.

4. Klezmer as Community

An earlier version of this chapter appeared as "Searching for the Klezmer city" in *Studies in Contemporary Jewry* 15 (1999), 35–48.

6. The Fiddler's Farewell

1. Hankus Netsky reports that old-time Philadelphia klezmorim told him the tune is from Ukraine, where it was known among non-Jews as "Plach, Yisroel," or "Cry, Israel," so its metamorphosis into a pleasantly poignant good-night waltz might be a nice case in point of Americanization of affect.

Works Cited

Auer, Leopold. 1921. *Violin Playing as I Teach it*. New York: Frederick A. Stokes.

Averill, Gage. 1994. "Mezanmi, Kouman Nou Ye? My Friends, How Are You? Musical Constructions of the Haitian Transnation." *Diaspora* 3/3:253–72.

Bach, C. P. E. 1753/1949. *Essay on the True Art of Playing Keyboard Instruments*, trans. W. J. Mitchell. New York: W. W. Norton.

Bauer, Susan. 1996. "Von der Khupe zum KlezKamp: Wandlungsprozesse und Formen der Reinterpretation von Klezmer-Musik in New York." M.A. thesis, Freie Universität, Berlin.

Baumann, Max, et al. 1986. *Klangbilder*. Berlin.

Bauman, Zygmunt. 1996. "From Pilgrim to Tourist—or a Short History of Identity." In *Questions of Cultural Identity*, ed. Stuart Hall and Paul du Gay. London: Sage, 18–36.

———. 1992. *Intimations of Postmodernity*. London: Routledge.

Berliner, Paul. 1994. *Thinking in Jazz: The Infinite Art of Improvisation*. Chicago: University of Chicago Press.

Boniface, Priscilla, and Peter J. Fowler, 1993. *Heritage and Tourism in "the Global Village"*. London: Routledge.

Brandes, Edda, et al., eds. 1990. *Klangbilder der Welt: Musik International in Berlin*. Berlin: Internationaler Institut fuer Vergleichenden Musikstudien und Dokumentation.

Brodkin, Karen. 1998. *How Jews Became White Folks and What That Says about Race in America*. New Brunswick NJ: Rutgers Unversity Press.

Bronson, Bertrand. 1969. *The Ballad as Song*. Berkeley: University of California Press.

Carson, Ciaran. 1996. *Last Night's Fun*. New York: North Point Press.

Cohen, Judith. 1997. "'Ay! Ribadavia': Re-creating Sephardic Culture in a Galician Town." *TRANSiberia*, an on-line journal.

Cowdery, James. 1990. *The Melodic Tradition of Ireland*. Kent, OH: Kent State University Press.

Dean, John, and Jean-Paul Gabilliet, eds. 1996. *European Readings of American Popular Culture.* Westport, CT: Greenwood Press.

Ebron, Paulla A. 1998. "Tourists as Pilgrims: Commercial Fashioning of Transatlantic Politics." Unpublished paper.

Fabre, Genevieve, and Robert O'Meally. 1994. *History and Memory in African-American Culture.* New York: Oxford University Press.

Feldman, Walter Zev. 1994. "Bulgareasca/Bulgarish/Bulgar: The Transformation of a Klezmer Dance Genre." *Ethnomusicology* 38/1:1–35. In Slobin 2000b.

———. 1997. Liner notes for *Fidl: Alicia Svigals, Klezmer Violin,* Traditional Crossroads CD 4286.

Fock, Eva. 1997. "Music—Intercultural Communication? Micro Musics, World Music, and The Multicultural Discourse." *Nordicom-Information* 4:55–65.

Frigyesi, Judit. 1996. "The Aesthetic of the Hungarian Revival Movement." In *Retuning Culture: Musical Changes in Central and Eastern Europe,* ed. Mark Slobin. Durham, NC: Duke University Press, 54–75.

Gebrider Moischele. 1995. CD album, *Schtil, di nacht is oisgeschternt.* Extraplatte EX 238-2.

Grossberg, Lawrence. 1996. "Identity and Cultural Studies—Is That All There Is?" In *Questions of Cultural Identity,* ed. Stuart Hall and Paul du Gay. London: Sage, 87–107.

Hall, Stuart. 1996. "Introduction." In *Questions of Cultural Identity,* ed. Stuart Hall and Paul du Gay. London: Sage.

Hammarlund, Anders. 1994. "Migrancy and Syncretism: A Turkish Musician in Stockholm." *Diaspora* 3/3:305–24.

Hemetek, Ursula, ed. 1996. *Echo der Vielfalt/Echoes of Diversity.* Vienna: Bohlau.

Kirshenblatt-Gimblett, Barbara. 1998a. *Destination Culture: Tourism, Museums, and Heritage.* Berkeley:University of California Press.

———. 1998b. "Sounds of Sensibility." *Judaism* 47/1:49–79. In Slobin 2000b.

Kroes, Rob. 1996. *If You've Seen One, You've Seen the Mall: Europeans and American Mass Culture.* Urbana: University of Illinois Press.

Lamasisi, Filip. 1996. "Musical Intercultural Encounters in Vienna: A Reflection on the Experience Associated with Performance of Ethnic Music of the Black Minority." In Hemetek 1996, 85–100.

La'om. 1997. Liner notes for . . . *spielt!* Raumer Records 11197.

Lauŝević, Mirjana. 1998. "A Different Village: Balkan Music in the United States." Ph.D. dissertation, Wesleyan University.

Mitchell, Tony. 1996. *Popular Music and Local Identity: Rock, Pop, and Rap in Europe and Oceania.* London: Leicester University Press.

Morson, Gary Saul, and Caryl Emerson. 1990. *Mikhail Bakhtin: Creation of a Prosaics.* Palo Alto, CA: Stanford University Press.

Netsky, Hankus. 1998. "Three Twentieth Century Jewish Musicians from Poland." Unpublished paper.

Neumann, Frederick. 1978. *Ornamentation in Baroque and Post-Baroque Music, with Special Emphasis on J. S. Bach.* Princeton, NJ: Princeton University Press.

Nora, Pierre. 1994. "Between Memory and History: Les Lieux de Memoire." In Fabre and O'Meally 1994, 284–300.

Ottens, Rita, and Joel Rubin. 1999. *Klezmer-Musik*. Kassel: Bärenreiter.

Quintillian. 1922. *The Institutio Oratoria of Quintillian*, trans. H. E. Butler. London: Heinemann.

Rasmussen, Ljerka Vidic. 1999. "Newly Composed Folk Music in Yugoslavia, 1945–1989." Ph.D. dissertation, Wesleyan University.

Rebling, Jalda. 1995. "Yiddish Culture—A Soul Survivor of East Germany." In *Speaking Out: Jewish Voices from Germany*, ed. S. Stern, Chicago edition q.

Ronstrom, Owe. 1992. *Att Gestalta Ett Ursprung*. Stockholm: Akadmitryck.

Roskies, David. 1984. *Against the Apocalypse: Responses to Catastrophe in Modern Jewish Culture*. Cambridge, MA: Harvard University Press.

Roth, Philip. 1959. *Goodbye, Columbus*. Boston: Houghton Mifflin.

Rothstein, Robert. 1998. "Klezmer-loshn.'" *Judaism* 47/1:23–28. In Slobin 2000b.

Rubin, Joel. 1998. "*Rumenishe Shtiklekh*: Klezmer Music among the Hasidim in Contemporary Israel." *Judaism* 47.1:12–22.

Salmen, Walter. 1991. . . . *denn die Fiedel macht das Fest: Jüdische Musikanten und Tänzer vom 13. bis 20. Jahrhundert*. Innsbruck: Edition Helbling.

Sapoznik, Henry. 1999. *Klezmer! Jewish Music from Old World to Our World*. New York: Schirmer Books.

Savigliano, Marta E. 1995. *Tango and the Political Economy of Passion*. Boulder, CO: Westview Press.

Schoenberg, Arnold. 1978. *Theory of Harmony*, trans. R. Carter. Berkeley: University of California Press.

Schuyler, Philip. 1984. "Berber Professional Musicians in Performance." In *Performance Practice: Ethnomusicological Perspectives*, ed. G. Behague, 91–148.

Slobin, Mark. 1982. *Tenement Songs: Popular Music of the Jewish Immigrants*. Urbana: University of Illinois Press.

———. 1984. "Klezmer Music: An American Ethnic Genre." *Yearbook for Traditional Music* 9:2–41.

———. 1988. "Icons of Ethnicity: Pictorial Themes in Commercial Euro-American Music. *Imago Musicae:* 129–43.

———. 1989. *Chosen Voices: The Story of the American Cantorate*. Urbana: University of Illinois Press.

———. 1994. "Music in Diaspora: A View from Euro-America." *Diaspora* 3.3:243–52.

———. 1996. "Bosnia and Central/Southeastern Europe: Musicians in Transition." In J. Titon, ed., *Worlds of Music* (3d ed.). New York: Schirmer Books, 211–51.

———. 1998. "The American Musical Landscape: Widening the Lens?" *Newsletter of the Institute for Studies in American Music* 18/2:1–2.

———. 2000a. *Subcultural Sounds: Micromusics of the West*. 2nd edition. Middletown, CT: Wesleyan University Press.

———. Ed. 2000b. *Klezmer Roots and Offshoots*. Berkeley: University of California Press.

Snodin, Michael, and Maurice Howard. 1996. *Ornament: A Social History since 1450*. New Haven, CT: Yale University Press.

Spottswood, Richard. 1990. *Ethnic Music on Records, 1893–1942*. Urbana: University of Illinois Press.

Statman, Andy. 1997. *Learn to Play Klezmer Music: Improvising in the Tradition*. Homespun Video.

Villa, Dana. 1996. *Arendt and Heidegger: The Fate of the Political*. Princeton, NJ: Princeton University Press.

Wong, Deborah. 1997. "Just Being There: Making Asian American Space in the Recording Industry," in *Musics of Multicultural America*, ed. K. Lornell and A. K. Rasmussen, New York: Schirmer Books, 287–316.

Yerushalmi, Yosef Haim. 1989. *Zakhor: Jewish History and Jewish Memory*. Seattle: University of Washington Press.

Contents of Accompanying CD

Variants of "Dem trisker rebns khosid"

1. Dave Tarras, September 1925, Columbia 8089-F. 3:25.
2. Alicia Svigals, *Fidl*, 1997, Traditional Crossroads CD 4826. Used by permission. 2:57.
3. Deborah Strauss, *The Singing Waltz*, 1997, Omega OCD 3027. Used by permission. 1:41.
4. Dave Tarras, *Dave Tarras: Master of the Jewish Clarinet*, 1978, Balkan Arts Center US 1002. Used by permission. 1:12.
5. Flying Bulgar Klezmer Band, 1999 (recorded 1996), Traditional Crossroads CD 4295. Used by permission. 3:13.

Variants of "Gas-nign"

6. Abe Schwartz, "National Hora," with Sylvia Schwartz, piano, ca. May 1920, Columbia E4745. 2:12.
7. Kandel's Orchestra, with Jacob Hoffman, xylophone, January 24, 1923, Victor 77018. 3:05.
8. Max Weissman, recorded as a trial, August 18, 1920, Victor GV 101. "Gas-nign" is the second half of the performance. 3:12.
9. Dave Tarras, *Dave Tarras: Master of the Jewish Clarinet*, 1978, Balkan Arts Center US 1002. Used by permission. 1:22.
10. Leon Pollak, *Ensemble Klezmer: Live in Prag*, 1997, Extraplatte EX 317-2. Used by permission. 2:20.
11. Deborah Strauss, spontaneous version recorded, 1997.
12. Alicia Svigals, *Klezmer Music: A Marriage of Heaven and Earth*, 1997, ellipsis arts, Roslyn LI CD 4090. Used by permission. 3:18.

13. Max Epstein band as "Dukes of Freilachland," *Mazeltov*, ca. 1960, AAMCO Records ALP 316. 2:42.

14. David Krakauer, recorded live at Tonic with David Krakauer's Klezmer Madness (Mark Stewart, electric guitar; Ted Reichman, accordion; Shahzad Ismaily, electric bass; Kevin Norton, drums), March 28, 1999. Used by permission of David Krakauer. 5:23.

15. Ran Blake, recorded live in New England Conservatory's Jordan Hall, 1991. Used by permission. 5:46.

Variants of "Araber-tants"

16. Naftule Brandwein, February 18, 1926, Victor 78658. 3:04.

17. La'om, " . . . *spielt! Klezmer-Musik von Chicago bis Odessa*," 1997. Raumer Records RR 11197. Used by permission. 5:05.

18. Hoo-Tza-Tza, *Hoo-Tza-Tza*, 1997, band-produced cassette. Used by permission. 8:52.

Index

diacritical marks, 106, 113, 127
diaspora, 6, 8, 9, 18–19, 21, 29–31, 82
dreydl, 76
dreydlakh, 112
drums, 70, 81, 82, 131
dybbuk, 68

early music, 63, 64, 65, 80, 83, 107
Elman, Mischa, 68
England, 58, 83
Epstein, Max, 50, 95, 96, 98, 99–100, 119, 125
Estonia, 18, 88
estrada, 72
ethnomusicology, 5, 9, 16–17, 18, 46, 67, 72–73, 93, 94

Fabre, Genevieve, and Robert O'Meally, 54, 55
Feidman, Giora, 56
Feldman, Walter Zev, 3, 96, 98, 99, 120, 121, 122, 123; writings of, 30, 93, 94, 97, 102, 108, 109, 129, 130
Fels, Gordon, 39
Festival of Jewish Traditions from the Former Soviet Union, 72
fiddle. *See* violin
Fiddler On The Roof, 23, 34, 73
Fidl (album), 98, 109–10, 125
Finns, 12, 20, 42
flute, 63, 68, 96, 110
folk music, 4, 20, 28, 41, 48–49, 50
foxtrot, 85
France, 26, 49
Frankel, Lt. Joseph, 4, 25, 34–35
Frontejas (album), 55

Gabriel, Peter, 41
Gagnon, Charles, 63
Gebirtig, Mordecai, 84, 85
Germans, 75, 82, 99
Germany, 16, 18, 23–24, 30–31, 56–59, 75, 82, 83, 84, 130, 131
Ginsburg, Mirra, 3
Global Village, 64, 128
Gojim, 88

goles, 29
Goodbye, Columbus, 70–71
gospel music, 125
Graetz, Irving, 122
Grammy Award, 18
Graz, 89
Greek music, 7, 108, 124
Greeks, 106, 129–30, 131
Greenman, Steve, 121
Grisman, David, 25
Groh, Mattias, 130
Grossberg, Lawrence, 136, 137
guitar, 50, 63, 81, 82, 87
Guzikov, Mikhail, 68

Hall, Stuart, 134, 135
Handbook of Irish Music, 106
Harow, Peter. *See* Horwitz, Joshua
Harry Kandel: Master of Klezmer Music (album)
Hartman, Glenn, 40
Hasidic Jews, 29–30, 62, 84, 87, 102, 111, 136
Hasidic music, 7, 55, 119
Hatić, Mensur, 18–19
Hawaiian music, 20, 28
heavy metal music, 48, 74
heritage, 4, 12–14, 30, 65, 85, 90
heritage music, 5, 14–21, 28, 30, 31–35, 63, 93, 119; marketing of, 38–39, 41
heritage system, 53, 54–55, 77, 95, 101
Hilyer, Raphael, 46
Hinojosa, Tish, 55
hip-hop, 20, 21, 74
History and Memory in African-American Culture, 54, 55
Hitler, Adolf, 57, 72, 135
Hodnik, Rudy, 40
Hoffman, Jacob "Jakie," 69, 124, 126
Hoffman, Joseph, 126–27
Holocaust, 22, 23, 57, 58, 61, 84, 85, 118
Hood, Mantle, 16
hora, 94, 123, 124, 126, 129
Horwitz, Joshua, 89, 96, 120
Hoyt, Peter, 120